See You in Two Weeks

Bruce Bishop

ESCARPMENT PUBLISHING

An adventure-travel memoir

See You in Two Weeks
Bruce Bishop
Copyright © 2022
Published by Escarpment Publishing,
Imprint of AIA Publishing, Australia.
ABN: 32736122056
http://www.escarpmentpublishing.com.au

Paperback ISBN: 978-1-922329-43-1

Introduction

For thirty years I worked alongside my wife Lindy leading tour groups in Australia and later in North America and Europe. Throughout this busy time, we dealt with numerous awkward and challenging situations, but the many life-changing experiences and fun times shared with people we met along the way far outnumbered any hiccups.

Just before the start of each tour, as we approached a bus stop or before opening a door into a meet-and-greet gathering, I kissed Lindy and said, 'See you in two weeks,' because, after the tour began, our passengers owned all our time, effort and attention.

Lindy and I enjoyed being engulfed by people sharing a passion for travel, and they frequently asked us to tell them about our own experiences. Our story-telling times usually ended in laughter, and people often suggested I should write a book for the enjoyment of our passengers or anyone else interested in travel. Our lifestyle of being constantly on the move intrigued them, and they wondered how we found and developed tours to so many unusual places. Very few understood that the two great loves of my life anchored this lifestyle. The first is the love I have for Lindy that probably started when I was about five years old, and the second is my love of the amazing machines that allowed us to do what we did.

I tell the story about how Lindy and I teamed up, blundered into the tour industry and struggled along until a simple, innocuous remark from my father steered us towards many successful years in adventure travel.

The following narrative is structured around the unique buses we used in each era, so there is some overlap of years when we operated machines in North America and Australia at the same time.

When thinking of the thousands of folks who toured with us over millions of kilometres in the dust and dirt of outback Australia, the mud and ice of the Canadian Arctic and later by bicycle, barge and on foot through Europe without any serious accident, we truly do give thanks. Only twice did we not arrive back on time and in the same tour vehicle in which we departed, although man and machine were challenged on many occasions.

A sincere thank you to all those who loyally supported and travelled with us over the years and especially to our family. Hopefully this book will help explain what we were doing during all those years when we were away from you.

Bruce Bishop

Bruce and Lindy in Yosemite NP, California, 2015.

1
How a Couple of Farm Kids Became Tour Operators

Even through weary eyes, the view from the driver's seat of my Mack truck was impressive. The long, wide bonnet with a silver bulldog bolted up the front pointed the way towards what the truckies called 'The Aeroplane', a series of steeply banked 'S' bends in the Hume Highway near Tarcutta, New South Wales. Sitting bolt upright and eager, I charged the thirty-eight-ton machine into these corners at full power to enjoy the sensation as the vehicle rolled and leaned its way through the bends while sounding like a jet with the turbocharger and tip turbine at full pitch. Whether this was flying or driving, as a twenty-seven-year-old driver, I found the thrills intoxicating.

Very few people understand what it's like to be unceasingly content in the driver's seat, but those who do, know how tight the bond can be between man and machine and that the thrill of driving can be addictive. That Mack and I were on the same wavelength. We worked together such that I could feel if it was operating comfortably or if something was wrong. I loved it to the point where I often patted it on the dash when overtaking a

Kenworth and sniggered how easily we could round up a wussey European MAN or Mercedes. Its function perfectly designed its classic form, so much so that the silver bulldog ornament on the front served as a grab handle to lift the bonnet.

Yes, I was addicted to driving, but I didn't understand why until years later. Apparently, according to science, a small number of people like me tend to live in the moment when driving and can easily reach that point of mindfulness that many others strive to achieve through meditation. When there, primary stress hormones are not released allowing us to relax and feel good, and anything making you feel good can be addictive. My mother sometimes expressed her non-scientific diagnosis. Whenever I spent long boyhood days out on the tractor, she rolled her eyes, shrugged her shoulders and said sympathetically, 'You've got the Duncan gene,' because all my Duncan cousins were just like me.

By my late twenties, I was married to the love of my life, Lindy, blessed with three robust young boys and revelling in the gruelling workload of life on the road. The Mack was a whopping upgrade from my father's old farm trucks that I drove when hauling hay and grain back to the family dairy farm near Berry on the South Coast of New South Wales. As a boy I always wanted to be a farmer, so after leaving school, I worked alongside Dad for seven years. But even though I loved the tractors, trucks and workshop tasks, I wasn't interested in cattle. Without ever intending to, I slowly became a full-time produce merchant and carrier when more and more neighbouring farmers asked me to supply hay and grain to them. This was good timing, because the family's priority at that time was no longer with the farm but tourism. Our property was where the first Europeans settled in the 1820s, and all the family's resources and interest were being directed towards restoring the ruins of the old penal settlement at Coolangatta.

Owning my first Mack in the mid-1970s put me among the new era of transport operators as the trucking industry transitioned out of the old era of slow and uncomfortable machinery to the new generation of high-powered equipment from the USA. By necessity, the old truckies were a rough, tough bunch driving terrible roads with no real support except from each other, so a very strong camaraderie and culture existed out on the highways and backroads. When two trucks met, the drivers always gave a friendly wave or just raised a finger off the steering wheel if too tired to wave. Breakdowns or flat tyres always saw someone stop to offer a helping hand, and a flash of headlights or an arm signal out the driver's window warned of any dangers ahead. I always felt a part of this culture even though I was of the new generation of driver and machine.

One cold winter's night and still four hours from home after a long day, I felt fidgety and restless in the driver's seat—the first signs of fatigue. Luckily, at the top of the next hill was a large area used by road-maintenance authorities to stockpile gravel, and truckies also used it as a rest area. I slowed the laden machine with the engine brake barking loud and lumpy, then swung off the highway and parked among a dozen or so trucks. The quietly idling engine brought relief after many noisy hours of driving, and my ears rang in the silence. The cold outside air jolted me awake as I climbed out of the warm cab and into the carnival-like atmosphere generated by hundreds of red, amber and clear lights ablaze on the parked trucks and the aroma of food being cooked. The truckies named this place 'Hotdog Hill', but a small yellow sign planted at the gate marked it as Stockpile Site 39. An enterprising old couple popularised it by selling hot food and drinks and providing a bonfire. This night they were doing brisk business, and perhaps a dozen drivers were standing around the fire with hands in pockets enjoying some crude banter. Normally I avoided these gatherings because I was always in a hurry, but tonight I needed to be near the warm fire while grabbing a bite for dinner and taking my mandatory half-hour rest break.

Most of the trucks parked nearby were single-drive prime movers hitched to spread-axle trailers with roped and canvas-covered loads. A nice little Mercedes 1418, very common at the time even though only capable of fifty-three miles per hour, stood beside a Japanese Nissan UD named the Hiroshima Screamer and a wide-bonneted Kenworth called Mackattacka.

An old unshaven bloke with grease-stained hands and wearing an army duffle coat that looked like the dog gave birth to pups on it defended his ageing English Foden from a cocky young Kenworth driver. 'Mate, she's an oldie and I own it,' he said, 'and besides, only Sheilas need power steering.'

The young Kenworth driver answered back smugly, 'It's a bloody miracle that the Poms won the war if that's the best they can make.'

They'd parked their trucks beside each other: the old English Foden from the 1960s with a Gardner 150 hp engine alongside what the future looked like, a new bogie drive Kenworth with a fourteen litre, 350 hp turbocharged and aftercooled engine. (Today's machines are 500–700 hp.)

CB radios added to the new truckie culture, and nearly all roads soon had their truckie names for various landmarks along the way. 'Logbook Hill' near Marulan was where drivers stopped to check paperwork before continuing through the truck-checking station, and the 'Biscuit' and 'Bottle' bridges in the Cullerin Range south of Goulburn marked where truck rollovers spilled loads of biscuits and bottles. Driving a truck through that range was difficult because both the Biscuit and Bottle railway overpass bridges were too narrow for oncoming trucks to meet and had sharp, blind-approach corners. Northbound trucks charged uphill towards these dangerous corners at full power to keep momentum on the climb, and drivers kept a keen ear on the CB radio to know what was coming the other way. The unwritten rule was that the truck pulling uphill had right of way, but there were no guarantees that all drivers knew this or that an oncoming truck had a CB radio. But the worst possible scenario was meeting a wobbling caravan.

Late one winter's night, I drove through there pushing hard to get back home to Lindy and the boys. The Mack ran amid a string of northbound machines climbing towards the railway overpass bridges in a thick fog. The gauges were all lit up on the Mack's wrap-around dash and, in that poor visibility, all I could see over the big bonnet were the taillights of the truck twenty-five metres ahead. The CB radio crackled with chatter as I split a half gear downshift and then, at full power, trustingly followed those taillights up the range and over the narrow bridges as fast as the Mack could go. I did this in a tired, almost robotic state of mind, and if the lead truck ran off the road, all of us strung out behind would have blindly followed. Later, when I realised how stupid and dangerous it was taking risks like that, I toned down my youthful confidence and forever after became 'Captain Safety' out on the highways.

~

My beloved R-Model Mack 1978.

I loved the trucking business and threw myself into it. We converted a shed on the farm into a small feed mill, and before too long had two trucks engaged supplying mixed stockfeed to many local dairies, but road taxes levied on every mile our trucks travelled hobbled our fledgling business. The government employed a team of ruthless auditors to ensure compliance, and we never knew when they would strike. One of these officials appeared unexpectedly at the front door, and Lindy invited him inside, not understanding how much I feared such a visit. I squirmed when she also asked him to join us for lunch and sat awkwardly as Shylock demanded his pound of flesh. For the first time, I witnessed Lindy's natural people skills in action as she disarmed him, and when departing, he gratefully said he'd never been treated so kindly before and wished us well in the future.

6

Perhaps she inherited or learned this from her parents. Her dad was the popular long-term mayor of the Shoalhaven, and her mum, using the same skills with which Lindy was blessed, supported him behind the scenes. It made no difference whether hosting a highfalutin bigwig or some poor bugger needing help, she knew instinctively how to make them feel at ease and welcome.

Lindy's family and mine shared a close friendship dating back to our grandparents in the 1930s. Our mothers were in the same class at school, and our fathers played football together and were active in the Berry community, so Lindy and I knew each other very well right from our earliest memories. I loved the times we spent together as kids, enjoying meals at each other's homes and days of fun on Seven Mile Beach. Lindy was a chubby little freckled-faced girl with dark, waist-length hair that she mostly tied back in plaits, and her broad smile lit up her whole face. She teased me and laughed at my silliness when I tried to impress her, but even at that very young age, we were very comfortable with each other.

When Lindy left school and applied for her first job at the Rural Bank, my father, Colin, wrote her a glowing character reference. She loved singing with a small group of girls at St Lukes in Berry, and on many occasions as we grew up, I enjoyed listening to them perform. But as the years passed, I confess to being distracted by how attractive she was, more so than how well they sang. One night while at a formal costumed ball, her father, dressed like the Duke of Wellington, took me aside and gave me a nudge to make the move because she'd just parted from her surfie boyfriend. I found it hard to take him seriously dressed as he was, but I'd often wondered if I had any chance with her because we were more like brother and sister—but how she'd changed. No more plaits or freckles, and her childhood chubbiness had turned into feminine curves, but still her radiant smile beamed happiness. Anyway, I took her father's advice.

We enjoyed the next couple of carefree years together, but when she travelled overseas with her two cousins, I missed her terribly. The only antidote to my loneliness was on the rugby field, where all the extra time I put into training paid off, and I was selected for Illawarra to play in the regional country competition. Almost a year after she came home, we married and set up house on the family farm. Lindy's smiling face greeted thousands of tourists in her new job as the district's assistant tourism promotions officer. We were soon blessed with our three sons, Thomas, Joseph and Andrew.

~

The stockfeed business was good for a few years, but the droughts of the early 1980s—when grain was in short supply, very expensive and customers slow to pay—brought us to our knees. We couldn't compete with the multinational feed companies, so we sought any other work for the trucks to help meet the massive lease payments. Our two Macks were both coupled to tri-axled aluminium tipper trailers, making them ideal for coal haulage, so we put them to work in the Illawarra, hauling coal down the mountain to the loader at Port Kembla. The two trucks were very similar, but I only ever drove the white one because, um, I don't know, it was just my truck. Two drivers and I worked a roster, keeping at least one truck working all the time on the coal and the second also when it wasn't hauling grain. I remember feeling exhausted but with no choice other than to keep running the rat race down the escarpment, doing battle with traffic and always in the filth of black-coal dust. Every chance we got for a departure from that job, we jumped at, particularly if it was for an interstate load, where a few days away from the endless loop of coal haulage provided a welcome reprieve.

Out on the highway, my beloved Mack could easily compete with the best of them, but not when hauling coal down the mountain, where it was much slower than the others. Not because we couldn't match them, but because we wouldn't. Most trucks careened down Mt Ousley at twice my speed, using engine brakes and service brakes until near the bottom, then drivers shifted into 'Mexican overdrive'—neutral—to propel them for a kilometre or so above their slow maximum-geared speed. Pungent burnt-brake smells were normal, but I just wouldn't drive like that and take those risks. Maybe it was the scare and wakeup call I gave myself that foggy night out on the Cullerin Range or, more likely, 'Silver' Euston's mentoring that made me so cautious.

Silver was one of those kinds of blokes you only meet occasionally through life, but he influenced me way more than he would've ever known. His real name was Noel, but everyone called him Silver because of his silver-grey hair, even at the age of forty. When we contemplated coal haulage, I sat with him for a week in his magnificent wide-bonneted Kenworth to learn all about the job. Silver impressed me with the immaculate presentation of his truck and himself. He dressed in ironed, olive-green King Gees, spoke in a deep reassuring voice and was unflappable in the saddle, so never felt the need to swear. He taught me how to make a quid out of trucking, when very few others could. Up till then no one other than my father showed me how to drive a truck, but many times I heard drivers say, 'You drive them like you hate them,' but that wasn't how Silver operated, and it took me just a few days to see how astute and clever he was. He loved his machine and drove it so smoothly and precisely that it just purred sweetly all day up hill and down dale.

His mastery of the gearstick made it seem as if it were standing in a bucket of soft butter rather than attached to a gnarly Road Ranger transmission that would punish any mistimed shift. The motto of less-skilled drivers using Road Ranger boxes was 'if you can't find it, grind it.'

Silver did five trips each day from Westcliff colliery down to the loader compared to seven by the rip, tear and bust operators. His routine for tipping loads was a little obsessive and compulsive; after tipping, he climbed out of the cab, grabbed some gloves and hearth brush from under his seat and swept any coal away from around the tailboard, then he brushed his boots off before getting back in. He put the gloves and brush neatly away, then picked up a flannel cloth and wiped the dash while getting the truck back underway. Sitting in the interior of that Kenworth was like being in the cockpit of a WWII bomber with rows of two-inch round gauges and toggle switches laid out on flat-steel dash panels. Silver wiped each one, every time. The Kenworth was immaculate, despite being six years old and having travelled the equivalent distance to that of going to the moon and back. Saturday mornings in the depot said it all. Silver greased the truck, gave it a wash and was back home to his big house by lunchtime, where he parked his equally immaculate F150 pickup truck in the garage beside his wife Kathleen's Holden Caprice. Back at the depot, everyone else frantically did maintenance and repairs all afternoon—replacing burnt brake linings, cracked brake drums, broken spring leaves and so on. Those blokes worked their tails off, but they all had the seats out of their pants.

Silver taught me about vehicle presentation, maintenance and steady safe driving. He would have been a brilliant coach operator, and in later years when Lindy and I morphed from trucks to buses, I always looked forward to meeting him along the road in his big green Kenworth and enjoying some CB radio banter with him. When driving a busload through the Illawarra, I usually kept the CB turned off because the truckies used a special dialect of English that I preferred my passengers not hear, but Silver was different, and when I spotted him, I turned on the CB.

'Copy in the K whopper, Silver,' I enquired on one occasion.

'Who's that?' came the crackled reply.

'The captain in the Bushy,' I frivolously replied.

'Captain! I'll tell you what a coach captain really is,' he exclaimed, 'it's a truckie in long socks.' He had my measure, because that's exactly what I was. 'See your Dragons struggled again this week,' he added, trying to provoke me.

'Sorry, mate, you're breaking up. Can't hear you. Catch you on the flip,' I said with a chuckle.

Like me, Silver took every opportunity to escape the Illawarra rat race by carrying anything other than coal. One wet day he headed to the Burrier Quarry west of Nowra for a load of blue metal. The narrow gravel road was very slippery where it ran high above the Shoalhaven River along what the truckies called 'The Rocks' section of the road. Tragically, his truck slipped off the edge and rolled down the near vertical slope into the deep water. Miraculously, Silver survived, but the Kenworth was wrecked. The trauma of the accident and the loss of the truck was more than he could cope with. Shortly afterwards, he suffered a massive heart attack and passed away. Incredibly, just months later Kathleen died in a light aircraft crash near Fitzroy Falls on the southern highlands of New South Wales.

⁓

After seven frantic years of effort supplying stockfeed to local dairy farms and hauling coal to stay afloat, the manager of the local dairy factory dropped in for a yarn. He rightly suspected we were stretched threadbare keeping up the crucial stockfeed supply to his shareholder farmers, and he offered to work with us to ease our burden. We did so and it worked very well to the point where we eventually sold our business to the Nowra Dairy Co-op at the same time as they bought another competitor. The three businesses were amalgamated, and I was employed to manage the combined produce divisions, but the trucks no longer had a role.

We sold the Mack in which I'd spent many years of my youth to someone in Victoria, and I lost track of it, but, even forty years later, some habits formed when driving it occasionally resurface. Recently, while driving my ute down the mountainous road into Kangaroo Valley late at night, I unconsciously leaned forward in the seat and reached for the engine brake switch on the dash as I must've done thousands of times before in the Mack.

For the first time in my adult life, work didn't involve having a steering wheel in my hands, and I felt that all the experience I'd gained was forever wasted. I didn't know it then, but the best was yet to come.

⁓

My first project at the co-op was to oversee the construction of a new stockfeed milling plant and modernise the retail produce section to be forklift friendly and allow retail customers to drive through for service. One of my former drivers, Slim Cartwright, recommended we employ his young mate, Bruno Corletto, recently out of the navy, to help him with the heavy work at the bagging machine. I thought long and hard about how I could put this young bloke to work with the larrikins at that place, knowing they would torment him over his Italian heritage. I called a meeting and asked, urged, even begged them to go easy on the new kid. When Bruno arrived, his approach blind-sided us.

At lunch on his first day, he opened a Tupperware dish containing left-over lasagne from his dinner the previous night and tucked in. As he ate, he said, 'Great wog food this stuff—makes the dago quick.' Then we heard all the wog jokes we ever knew.

It left us speechless, but there was a collective sigh of relief in the room.

Bruno fitted in right from day one, and today, forty years later, he is still one of my best mates, having worked alongside us on tour operations for much of this time.

After a few days on the bagging machine, I promoted him to the retail driveway, where he quickly introduced some big and necessary changes. Our customers were accustomed to getting blunt treatment and somewhat rude jokes, particularly from old Ray O, who knew most of them well enough to get away with the terrible things he said. One time, I overheard him serving a regular customer who wanted a large bag of dog food and he asked her, 'Do you want to eat it here or take it away?'

Bruno was good for business and brought a level of service and hospitality never seen before in a produce store. He greeted every customer with enthusiasm, calling them sir or madam, then ran to quickly fill their order. If the ladies needed to get out of their vehicles, he opened the car door for them and addressed them as ma'am. News spread around the district about this young bloke at the feed store, bringing in many customers just to see what all the fuss was about. I kept an eye on the drive-through from my office window and often chuckled at the things I saw Bruno do to please them. One day he was serving a mature-aged lady and speaking to her in Italian. She was clearly enjoying this, so he jumped up onto a pallet of bagged feed with a broomstick, pretending to be a Venetian gondolier, and broke out with a rousing rendition of 'O Sole Mio'.

Bruno's talents were wasted in that job, so I was delighted when my brother Greg poached him away for the Coolangatta Estate. There he worked full-time in hospitality and eventually became the 'singing barman' in the regular Bush Banquet dinner shows that were very popular at the time. Bruno met his future wife, Christine, while working at the estate. She later spent thirty years running our tour office.

During the four years working at the co-op, I enjoyed jogging to keep fit, even though I no longer played rugby. Sometimes I ran the steep logging track to the top of Mt Coolangatta, which stands one thousand feet above sea level at the back of the family farm. At the summit after an exhausting half-hour slog, I always stopped to regain my breath and enjoy the stunning view. Who knows how long I spent up there each time, but I always found something interesting to watch down below, like the pounding surf along the ocean shores of Seven Mile Beach, tractors working in the patchwork of paddocks or even the distinctive peak of Pigeon House Mountain eighty kilometres distant. The name Coolangatta is the anglicised version of the Aboriginal name Cullenghutti, which means 'great view'.

I began to think that if we could find a practical method of driving sightseers up there, surely it would be a good local attraction and would provide extra income for our young family. Any machines capable of climbing the thirty-five-degree grades safely were ridiculously expensive, so we baulked at taking the risk. But the driving addiction that compelled me to spend my childhood out on the tractor and years behind the wheel of a semitrailer raised its ugly head. The more I contemplated the concept, the more my longing for the thrills and excitement of owning and driving such a machine tainted my judgement.

I discussed some ideas with an old truckie mate, Kerry Rumble, and he offered to build the machine for me. Two truckies on a mission scrounged the yard, workshop and newspaper ads for components and 'designed' the machine around what we found. An ex-WWII Chev Blitz, some tractor wheels, a set of second-hand seats from an old government bus and a cheap garbage truck in South Australia. Kerry started fabricating a makeshift roll frame and assembling components together while I flew to South Australia to get the garbage truck, which would provide the engine and transmission. On the long trip back, it broke down briefly in Yass. The local garbage contractor spotted it and bought the compactor body, paying more for it than the truck cost. We painted the finished project Caterpillar yellow just like any proper machine and gave it the corny name of Bigfoot to appeal to the kids. Thankfully, at that time it required very little government compliance to operate on our own property.

Bingo, in 1982 we entered the adventure tourism business.

Bigfoot on the mountain summit, 1982.

Bigfoot tours became a very popular and iconic local tourist attraction. In its last full year of normal operation, we carried 20,000 plus passengers. My old mate Bruno Corletto drove the very last tour to the mountain summit in March 2021.

Often, after driving Bigfoot tours, passengers asked if we did any other trips with the giant machine, but it was three metres wide and unregistrable for travel on public roads. Encouraged by the interest and driven by my insatiable quest for another machinery 'hit', we commissioned the building of a registerable version of the Bigfoot, despite not knowing how we would pay for it. The Snowmobiles on the Columbia Icefields in the Rockies of Alberta, Canada, inspired the design, and John Callaghan, a very experienced motor-body builder, agreed to build it for us. All I gave him to work from was a pencil sketch and several Snowmobile photos. The first time I met John, he was cutting a Rolls Royce Silver Shadow in half with an angle

16

grinder ready for conversion into a stretched limousine, so he had my confidence. He created our Bushmobile six-wheel drive bus alongside some magnificent Rolls Royce, Ford Ltd and Cadillac stretched limos, though it shared nothing in common with them. Our Bushmobile was an immensely capable off-road cross between a bus and a tractor.

Just weeks after we'd finished the new bus, the bus industry in New South Wales was deregulated, so I entered the bus industry only needing to gain a Diploma of Coach Management. This took several weekends of tuition at the University of Sydney's Business School, where I sat the course with the first group of operators to do so. What I learned was useful, but making many industry contacts was invaluable.

In 1988 we entered the bus industry.

Business hummed during this period, so we took another opportunity to increase our involvement in tourism by purchasing the old railway fettler's barracks beside the railway station in Bomaderry. The barracks had ten guest rooms plus a spacious lounge with a fireplace and reasonable kitchen and bathroom facilities. We established a backpackers' hostel furnished with items bought cheaply at government auctions and gained affiliation with the Youth Hostels Association of Australia (YHA).

~

Australia's bicentennial year was an exciting time to be in tourism. Hoges was slipping another shrimp on the barbie in the USA, and international visitors flooded down to say g'day. Backpacking was a big part of Australia's tourism product, and this filled us with enthusiasm in these confident times.

Every Friday afternoon we did a 'milk run' in the

Bushmobile to pick up passengers around the Sydney YHA backpacker hostels for a three-day-weekend package tour into the Shoalhaven district. As intended, the big yellow bus attracted a lot of attention, so we were promoting as well as transporting. The young passengers always gasped at how beautiful our part of the world was and were astonished by the absence of crowds.

Adapting from rural industries and trucking to inbound tourism with all its hidden lures and traps was a steep learning curve. At the time, a thriving demand for short, packaged tours from Sydney's four-star hotels existed, and we spent months delving into and trying to understand what really drove that market. As newcomers, we had no idea who was in the pockets of whom and where we could find trustworthy associates. To our horror, we uncovered a marketplace corrupted by some operators who paid cash commissions to hotel reception staff for recommending and booking their products. This scene wasn't for us, but it drove us on our quest for a product so unique that it would stand out amidst all the competition.

The highlight of every backpacker tour we brought into the Shoalhaven was a visit to the abandoned gold mines at Yalwal, nestled in a beautiful valley thirty kilometres west of Nowra. Access into the cliff-fringed valley took us down a road built for bullock wagon use back in the mid 1850s and past a large dam that created a lake for several kilometres back into the valley. I led walks by torchlight into the old mine tunnels, and Lindy served picnic lunches followed by fresh damper and tea. Our go-anywhere Bushmobile bus got us to places where no other bus could go—across creeks and rivers, to isolated scenic outlooks and to where wildlife spotting was assured. Many local schools soon saw the educational potential and booked school excursions to the mines. We modified those itineraries to fit into a regular school day and operated seventy trips to Yalwal in the first year.

Often backpackers joined school groups, giving them an experience like no other. One time we hosted a German fellow who was a bit of a character, so we dressed him as a bushranger, and Lindy drove him out along the Yalwal road and hid him in the bush ready to hold up the bus full of ten-year-old school kids. The bus was quite late that morning, and the young German, hiding in the bush on his own in the middle of nowhere, must have questioned himself. When the bus came around the corner, he sprang out of hiding and stood in the middle of the road with water pistols pointing at us before bursting aboard yelling above all the squeals, 'Give me please all your lollies.'

The big yellow bus only ever got stuck out there once, but only because wet grass caused it to slip sideways on a very steep hill. The local Volunteer Bush Fire Brigade came to my aid willingly and towed it back onto the track free of charge but then asked if we wanted to buy some raffle tickets—ten books!

Lindy and I were off to a brilliant start in our new life working together in adventure tourism and happily doing business with interesting people from all over the world. What a change from stockfeed and trucking, where customers were so reluctant to spend money that they would sell their souls to save a buck.

All our planning, investment, risk taking and hard work soon crashed to a halt when authorities closed off all public vehicular access to a vast area of the ranges, including the area of the mines.

What the heck could we do with this machine now?

2
Stumbling and Fumbling into Outback Touring

At that point, we were heavily in debt and the national economy was struggling. Our backpacker hostel and Bigfoot attraction were barely paying their way but keeping us tied down, and the bus business has just been locked out of the destination it had been purposely built to access.

On the positive side, though, a constant stream of backpackers came through and shared stories of their Australian and world travels, which triggered the urge within us to travel and see for ourselves. Even though never profitable, on reflection, this business was the best thing for Lindy, the boys and me. We learned how to enjoy the simpler things and to just open our eyes and look at all the wonderful things around us.

In an atlas, I marked with little notes places where special people came from and we dreamed of visiting ourselves one day. We also hung a large world map on the wall and invited each guest to place a coloured pin on the map where they lived. The largest number of pins sat on Germany, then the UK, USA, Canada, Scandinavia, Japan, New Zealand and South Korea.

At our Bomaderry hostel, we attracted the more adventurous backpackers. When asked why they headed south of Sydney, the usual answer was, 'Because the crowds are going north.'

A young Bavarian fellow named Josef Stigler was our most memorable backpacker. After six months in Australia, he was filling in a couple of weeks before flying back home to his little rural village. Within days, Lindy, myself and our boys became very fond of him. A bricklayer by trade, he enjoyed his visit to the fullest, starting off by buying a motorbike and riding solo around the country. The bike broke down in South Australia, so he bought a Mini Moke to finish his travels. When he arrived in Bomaderry, he'd learned basic English and some Aussie sayings.

Early one morning I saw Jo cleaning the Moke ready to sell, and he asked for my help to 'de-blood the brakes'. We both cracked up when I said, 'I think you mean bleed the brakes, Jo.'

A buyer dropped in to buy it, and I later asked Jo if he'd sold it. 'I lost the ship with that buyer,' he replied, scrunching his face.

'Lost the ship?' I asked. 'Oh, you mean missed the boat, mate.'

Jo did jobs around the hostel for his keep, and we adopted him into our family. When we drove him to Sydney Airport for his departure, we left him with empty hearts.

As he said he would, Jo returned to us several times over the next few years and even brought his mother and sisters out from Germany to meet us. We could barely communicate with them, but formed a very warm and fond connection. Jo ended up marrying an Australian girl and settling here. He fitted in perfectly and bought a ready-mix concrete plant in Cootamundra and later a trucking business on the central coast. Sadly, he became ill and passed away, leaving a wife and three young children.

Many years later, we visited the Stigler family in Bavaria,

and they treated us like royalty. Family members, many of whom we'd met in Australia, travelled from afar to meet us, and their hospitality was extraordinary. We walked with them around their little rural village of Gunching feeling like we'd been there before, but perhaps it was because Jo had told us so much about it. In the village centre stood a beautiful medieval Catholic church with Jo's photo on a memorial. We all teared up and hugged.

We hosted hundreds of young, adventurous people from all over the world who wanted to share their travel experiences and meet other young people. Many senior folks also came through, seeking the simpler things in life, even though they could afford whatever they wished. University professors, business people, walking groups, sporting groups, birdwatchers and so on. We were the nearest YHA hostel to Sydney, the gateway to Australia, so at Bomaderry we welcomed either those starting their Australian adventure or those filling in a couple of days before departing.

Living and working in such an interesting and stimulating situation was good for our family. Our biggest dilemma was how to avoid financial ruin and utilise the big 6WD tour bus sitting out the front. Where else could we use it?

A political controversy hit the news when the New South Wales government granted a commercial licence to AAT Kings, one of Australia's leading tour companies, that gave them exclusive access to an area in the Blue Mountains. The tour involved taking a 4WD coach through the exclusion zone around the Warragamba Dam, Sydney's primary water supply, to a place called Yerranderie, where silver was mined in the early 1900s and two thousand people once lived. The town became a ghost town when the construction of the Warragamba Dam cut off all practical road access.

We decided to go and find Yerranderie for ourselves, so we borrowed a Landcruiser from Lindy's sister Sally. Knowing it was impossible to gain access through the Burragorang Valley like AAT Kings, we explored options from the western side, hoping to find an adventurous route with good scenery and wildlife spotting. Boy, did we find it! From Mittagong to the Wombeyan Caves Reserve passing through a tunnel and along a very narrow road cut into the steep valley walls with precipitous drop-offs, then via the Limeburners Fire Trail and historic Oberon–Colong stock route into Yerranderie.

That night we stayed in the old post office lodge building and met the elderly owner, Val Lhuede, one of the most impressive people we ever met. Val had a small flat upstairs where she often stayed when visiting, but her main home overlooked Sydney Harbour at Kirribilli. She talked for hours, telling funny stories like the time she visited Hermannsburg Mission near Alice Springs in the early 1950s and unknowingly sat on a wooden toilet seat just painted by Albert Namatjira. She bragged that Australia's best known indigenous artist had painted her butt. In many ways she was ahead of her time, having travelled the world in the post war period and pursued a career in architecture. She lived for a while on a houseboat moored in Sydney's Middle Harbour before selling it to John Singleton, a very wealthy advertising and media entrepreneur, who then lived onboard himself for a short time.

Hiking from Katoomba to Mittagong as a young person had sparked the passion that led her to spend most of her life and wealth dedicated to salvaging the buildings and history of Yerranderie. Like many others doing this trek, she stopped overnight at the abandoned town and camped in the decaying buildings. She'd been there before with her father when he invested in a consortium seeking to reopen the mines, but the scheme failed when access was lost. Val made a commitment to save as much as she could, starting by buying her father's share and any other portions that ever came up for sale.

Road access was difficult, so she joined forces with Neville Lang, a nearby landowner, and bought a bulldozer to make the old stock route trafficable to four-wheel-drive vehicles. The dozer also blazed an airstrip near the old town, so then goods and services could come by road, and Val and her future customers could fly in from Picton. Over the next few years, she established 'eco' accommodation well before anyone else grasped the concept.

Yerranderie excited us, and we knew from what we'd learned from travellers at the hostel that this was, indeed, a very special place. The astonishing scenery of Bartlett Head, rising six hundred feet vertically behind the old town and, above that, Yerranderie Peak at three thousand feet, gave the town an impressive backdrop. Looking east from the old post office lodge veranda, you could see the Burragorang Walls across the waters of Warragamba Dam, and to the north, Burns Saddle dipped between the cliff faces of Colong point and the Axehead mountain. In the daytime, huge goannas lurked around the old town, and later in the day, mobs of grey kangaroos grazed in the main street and among the buildings. For the more energetic visitor, a walking trail to the top of the Yerranderie Peak rewarded them with a view of the lights of Sydney after dark. Although most of the old town's buildings had fallen victim to the ravages of time, the post office, Mrs Barns' Guest House, Sam Meldrum's tailor shop, Slippery Norris's residence, Woodhill's store, the police station, court house and Catholic church survived. Numerous abandoned mines and rusting machinery lay deserted everywhere, and it felt as if civilisation was thousands of miles away—but we were only sixty miles from the GPO in Sydney.

The rich story about the silver discovery and mining added to the splendid scenery. A farmer digging post holes found the silver ore body, and after that, large-scale mining operated around the clock for six days each week. When all the machinery stopped at midnight on Saturday nights, the deafening silence woke the town. Mining prospered until WWI, then declined steadily until the great Wall Street collapse of October 1929 when plummeting silver prices forced most to close down.

That first night at Yerranderie, knowing we'd found the perfect destination for future tours that offered everything we sought and was close enough to home to be feasible, we could hardly sleep for excitement.

Over the next thirty years, we took thousands of people to Yerranderie, and this established our future in adventure touring.

~

Though the first tour went well, we faced two big problems. A huge boulder had tumbled down the mountainside and blocked Wombeyan Caves Road. It was too heavy to drag away with a chain, straddling it wasn't an option, and the road was too narrow to drive around it, especially with a drop of several hundred feet vertically into the river valley below. Going back the way we came required reversing for several kilometres to a turnaround space, and we were already running late. The boulder was about two metres square and half a metre high, so I hatched a plan. With our Bushmobile in 6WD low range, I engaged low gear, the giant lugged wheels grabbed onto the rock, and we simply drove right up and over it. This machine was more tractor than bus, but I hadn't anticipated how terrifying it must have been for the passengers seated on the right-hand side as the bus leaned precariously over the cliff edge. It reminded me of a documentary film I'd seen about the nightmarish drive over the Andes mountains in Bolivia along the highway to hell.

I noticed the second problem when we arrived at Yerranderie. A power-steering hose was leaking fluid, and I didn't have a spare. Luckily, just minutes before, a Cessna had landed on the gravel airstrip nearby, so I arranged with the pilot to fly me to Camden airport where the Pirtek man was waiting to make a new hose. Within a couple of hours, I'd repaired the machine, and a massive grin hid my relief.

~

At the beginning of our tours to Yerranderie, we used the multi-share accommodation in the renovated old post office building, and Lindy prepared all meals in the small kitchen. What the destination lacked in comforts, it made up for with all the other highlights, especially the views. In later years our groups stayed in a motel in Oberon, and we travelled down and back in a day via the stock-route track.

Once we took a booking from a Probus Club who wished to travel in just two weeks' time, but at such short notice, the little budget motel in Oberon had no rooms available. The more upmarket motel had rooms, however, and the owner 'Big Kev' McGrath, understanding our predicament, charged the same rate as the budget motel on that occasion. The group was ecstatic, and we saw how quality lodgings made people much happier, so for the next twenty-five years we patronised the Big Trout Motel and formed a strong friendship with Big Kev, Stella and the extended McGrath family.

Kev was also a farmer, who worked closely with his brother, Anthony, sharing ownership of the farm and motel. Often, he invited us to visit the woolshed, where either he or Anthony demonstrated sheep shearing. Before arrival I always told the story of the two brothers and how they worked together on the farm and motel, wherever the need was greatest. Kev met us at the woolshed one time, and after finishing shearing, raced home, showered and was behind the bar as the group arrived for dinner on their first night. Many assumed he was the other brother, causing gossip all night on how alike the brothers were. Even Kev thought it was funny and played along by badmouthing his brother Kevin.

Down at Yerranderie Val was often in residence when we brought groups in, but she always had a caretaker/guide to look after us and keep the groups entertained. Over the years all caretakers became somewhat eccentric, and we often discussed whether the isolation of the job caused it.

Merlin the Nebraskan had a wife so starved of retail opportunity that she shopped for items in Val's gift shop, then nearly always returned them next day. And Dave the Yowie enjoyed catching goannas by the tail to frighten onlookers.

John and Lyn Hopwood were another good example as their behaviour became more unusual with the passing of time. They stumbled upon Yerranderie when trekking nearby on the Bicentennial National Trail. The trail is a multiuse recreational route stretching 5,330 kilometres from Cooktown in Far North Queensland to Healesville in Victoria. For six months they travelled the trail, leading a coffle of six donkeys that carried all their equipment and supplies. At Yerranderie they rested for several days, formed a strong bond with Val and accepted her offer of full-time employment as caretakers.

They stayed for several years and had two children (without TV reception), but after finding a goanna in the cot with the baby, they felt they needed to move. However, they often returned to help when subsequent caretakers took holiday breaks. I looked forward to catching up with them—if for no other reason than to see what John would get up to for the night, because he enjoyed a drink more than most. A well-educated Englishman, he spoke with a posh Cambridge accent and always wore a Khaki shirt, Bombay Bloomer shorts and sometimes even a white pith helmet just like Sir Sidney Ruff-Diamond in *Carry on up the Khyber*. While seated at the dinner table, he sarcastically whinged about everything imaginable before opening a bottle of wine and proposing his favourite toast: 'Better to have a bottle in front of me than a Frontal Lobotomy.'

Our most satisfying trip to Yerranderie was with an elderly passenger and former resident of the town, who was returning for the first time since her mid-teens. Stella was in her late eighties and travelled with her daughter and granddaughter, hoping to show them where her childhood home had stood, even though it was long gone. I stopped the bus alongside the track near where she suggested, and everyone on the bus walked with her as she pushed through the thick scrub energetically like a much younger woman. Once in the vicinity of her old home, she asked us all to search for a seat-shaped rock where she'd often sat for hours at a time pondering what her future life in the outside world might hold for her. Incredibly, we found it, along with a heap of stone, once the fireplace and chimney of the house. Three generations of girls became very emotional and couldn't thank us enough for facilitating such a special moment for them.

~

We became somewhat more ambitious after a few successful Yerranderie tours and planned an exploratory trip to the most northerly point in Australia on Queensland's Cape York Peninsula. Lindy was not convinced that an eight thousand kilometres return trip was a good idea and raised some good questions. Was our bus capable of doing such a long trip when it was built to just poke along on short local tours? Who would run the hostel for four weeks when we couldn't afford to pay ourselves, let alone somebody else? Would the boys be okay with us gone? Even though they were old enough to look after themselves, they were young enough to get up to plenty of mischief. Who would look after the dog that was inclined to wander? What would we do if the bus let us down? No way could we afford a replacement.

To all the above, I replied, 'I don't know.'

Anyway, we still did it.

We set off with fifteen spirited souls aboard, all knowing that we'd never been up to the Cape before, that we wouldn't be following a fixed itinerary and had only an approximate return-by date. The one thing they did know, however, was that we calculated the tour price to just cover costs.

Several passengers on board were over eighty years old, and everyone else was in their seventies, except for Graham Davis, who was about our age and had worked with Lindy in her first job at the Rural Bank. The only other people we knew before departure were retired naval Commander Ken Douglas and his wife Brenda.

If we'd known what lay ahead of us as we left Bomaderry early on that first day, we would've stayed at home in bed.

Our close connection to the YHA organisation gave us a perfect choice of budget accommodation, and wherever a YHA hostel wasn't available, we camped. Everyone brought their own camping equipment and manhandled it down the aisle of the bus to stow it across the back two rows of seats, along with the catering supplies and equipment. The bus had no storage bins underneath like conventional vehicles, so it was hard work for us all the way.

Challenges were a daily event. Luckily, in all those years running the trucks, I developed a habit of inspecting the vehicle with a walkaround every time we stopped and more thoroughly at night by getting underneath for a real good look. That first night in Segenhoe, I noticed a problem with a brake line that required urgent attention. First thing next morning we stopped in Scone for Lindy to do some restocking and for the passengers to have a walk. When everyone was out of sight, I removed the brake line and had it repaired. When they returned, I was casually sipping a coffee. I never told them.

As we pressed on up the hilly New England Highway, it quickly became apparent that, lacking engine horsepower and highway gearing, our machine was out of its depth for long-distance travel. In four weeks, we overtook one vehicle—an old Ford F600 farm truck overloaded with bagged potatoes. We all gave a loud and enthusiastic cheer as we went past.

The few days we spent on Fraser Island—the largest sand island in the world and just a few miles off the Queensland coast—gave us the chance to justify to all aboard that travelling on our bus had some advantages despite it being slow. It was the first time we'd taken a bus on a beach, and it was exhilarating for all aboard, especially when a light aircraft flew low overhead and landed on the beach in front of us. The big 6WD made easy work of sandy bush tracks where many less-capable vehicles struggled. It got us to where the magnificent forests of giant hoop pines thrived and to crystal-clear freshwater lakes away from the crowds. We saw the area mined for rutile—a titanium mineral—decades before and forestry camps abandoned when national parks management replaced forestry. Everywhere we drove, we became the centre of attention, and the passengers seemed to enjoy this.

The wreck of the Cherry Venture on Teewah Beach, Queensland.

After the first five days, we started to bond as a happy team, and I became cautiously confident in the machinery. This confidence was soon shattered, however. Late on the day we left Fraser Island, the bus transmission seemed to neutralise. Thankfully, we had enough momentum to roll into a nearby truck-parking bay and, luckily, the 'brick' mobile phone was just in range. We phoned for a local bus to collect the group along with their luggage and take them into Rockhampton. Lindy went with the group and left me and Graham to guard the disabled machine.

Graham and I had a terrific night around the campfire with

as many sausages as we could eat and plenty of cold beer. At sunrise next morning, a Detroit Diesel/Allison mobile service van and mechanic arrived. We removed the Allison transmission, replaced the broken flex plate coupling and re-installed the transmission in about eight hours. Later, when we caught up with Lindy and the group in Rockhampton, they met us like heroes with applause and special treats at dinner.

The passengers became frivolous. One of the older ladies found a squashed and dried cane toad beside the road and put it in Graham's bed. The problem was that she mistakenly put it in retired naval Commander Ken Douglas's bed, and he suspected Graham was the culprit. Thankfully for Graham, he wasn't at sea aboard Commander Douglas' warship, because surely he would've been court-martialled, sentenced and keelhauled. After several days, Molly confessed and cleared the air.

The real adventure for us started north of Cairns. The roads were rough and corrugated beyond anything we'd ever seen before, and the fine dust penetrated every conceivable place. The trip became a nightmare for us and the machine. At Lakeland Downs village near Cooktown, we struck trouble. The thrashing dealt to the bus by the terrible roads caused the soldered joint around a fuel-tank filler cap to crack. Diesel fuel splashed out and caused dust to cling to the wet area, making mud that risked contaminating fuel in the tank. Most people think of Cape York as being tropical and lush, and it is along the east coast where the mountainous Great Dividing Range blocks inland movement of rain-bearing cloud. Elsewhere it's quite dry with poor soils that only support grassland and scattered woodland. The big exception to this is on the fertile red-soil country around Lakeland Downs where several peanut farmers from Kingaroy moved to grow peanuts in the 1960s. The good news for us was the substantial mechanical workshop situated there, so I worked alongside a mechanic until midnight to fix the problem. We drained the fuel and piped exhaust gases from his ute into the tank so volatile fumes wouldn't blow our heads off while soldering it.

We learned quickly how to pack supplies, especially things like canned beer and soft drink. If not tightly packed, the cans rubbed together and leaked their contents onto the cardboard boxes that then disintegrated, allowing the cans to roll all through the bus. Dust then turned to sticky, sugary mud.

We also learned that it's hard to please all people all of the time. One passenger had just given me a compliment on the way we were so casual with timing when another came along tapping her watch face, wanting us to become more regimented. Other requests differed—turn the music up, or turn the music down; the bus is too hot, or the bus is too cold. We needed to learn diplomacy quickly.

The Peninsula Development Road branched northward from Lakeland Downs, and a big warning sign gave the distance to Weipa—580 kilometres. At the workshop on the previous night, the mechanic suggested we deflate the tyres a bit to soften the impact on the corrugations, and the difference was astounding. We reduced the pressure from ninety pounds per square inch to fifty in the huge super single tyres, so instead of driving what felt like a jackhammer, the machine padded over the bumps quite well. The poorly maintained gravel road rarely allowed speeds above sixty kilometres per hour because we needed to negotiate the regular sharp dips into gullies cautiously, and steep jump-ups onto low wooded ridges slowed progress. Occasionally, the landscape changed from undulating savannah woodlands to vast expanses of treeless black-soil plains where axle-busting ditches lay hidden deep underneath fine bulldust. Countless termite mounds resembling graveyard headstones dominated the featureless landscape all the way to the horizon, and waterholes had signs warning of saltwater crocodile danger.

We enjoyed a welcome reprieve from the relentless rough roads in Coen, a former gold mining outpost of several hundred people, mostly Aboriginal. While our passengers strolled the main street—just a pub, a store and a mechanical workshop— we overheard Molly say in a loud voice, 'I like the black ones.' Afraid that she'd caused offence, we looked towards the voice and discovered that she and her travel partner, Kit, were simply sorting through a bag of jellybeans.

Having never been up to the top before, it was difficult to know how far to go on each leg because we had no idea what the track conditions were like or what facilities we'd find along the way. Every so often we came across some amazing sights, like a massive railway bridge near Laura built in the 1890s with five 80-foot steel trusses on concrete piers fifty-five feet above the Normanby River. This was part of a railway intended to link Cooktown with the Palmer River Goldfields but never completed. North of Coen, we discovered a substantial airfield built during WWII as an advanced operational base for US bombers, and a crashed USAAF Douglas C47 transport plane lay in the scrub beside the track near Bamaga. At one point we drove for several hours through the scrub without knowing if we were going the right way. Numerous tracks formed a braided pattern, but all headed in the right general direction.

At the Wenlock River crossing, the water was only about three feet deep, so it presented little challenge for our large bus. However, as we set up camp on the riverbank, we watched with fascination as the deep water flooded a young fellow in a 4WD when about halfway across. Thankfully some other travellers towed him out because the river was a saltwater crocodile habitat, and no way was I going to wade in to help. Nearby was the historic Morton telegraph station built in the late 1880s as one of six repeater stations on the overland telegraph line between Thursday Island and Laura, where it linked with the existing system. A corridor forty metres wide was cleared through the bush for the poles and wires, and a bridle track developed alongside, enabling access for line maintenance and the opening of grazing and mining opportunities on the Cape. The first motor vehicles followed this route and, one hundred years later, it's still in use as a challenging alternative to the new bypass road.

We drove sections of each route, but on the Telegraph Track, we couldn't fit the bus under low-hanging branches without using the chainsaw, and we baulked at risking the near-impossible crossing of Gunshot Creek, so we returned to the bypass road. Further north and back on the Old Telegraph Track, we easily crossed Broken Axle Creek and continued to Twin Falls, where we set up camp. Enormous volumes of clear, fresh water flowed from the coastal mountains and poured over the low, wide falls, creating natural spa pools with safe swimming in the absence of crocodiles. As the sun set, a cacophony of bird calls erupted, led by the blue-winged kookaburra that just couldn't quite get the laugh right or maybe didn't have the same sense of humour as that of the laughing or eastern kookaburra. My favourite was the bar-shouldered dove with the most beautiful 'Cook-a-wook … cool-li-coo' melody.

Driving bush tracks put unreasonable strain on the machine and on me, as I knew that all those adventurous souls were relying on us. One day, without any warning, an unusual noise from an unknown source joined the other constant rattles, squeaks and thumps. Fear of a developing problem gripped me. It continued all afternoon and concern increased to despair by not having any clue as to the cause. It wasn't a rotational or impact noise, nor was it from the engine or transmission, and it happened randomly at varying volumes.

Later in the afternoon, a passenger exclaimed, 'Will you stop making that silly noise please, Ted. It's driving us all nuts.'

Eventually, during a miserable afternoon with a fierce gale blowing, we reached the Aboriginal and Islander communities near the top and camped at Red Island Bend (later called Seisia). Sand blasted the campground, and frequent torrential rain squalls belted through, so all we could do was hunker down as best we could. That night was the only time Lindy ever offered 'truckie scones' (Weet-Bix, jam and cream) for dessert—all other options just weren't possible.

Next day, we drove forty kilometres further north and set up camp in the sheltered campground beside the Wilderness Lodge Resort just several hundred metres from the northernmost point of mainland Australia. We all felt a great sense of achievement as we walked over the rocky headland leading to the sign that read 'You are standing at the most northerly point of mainland Australia'. Corks from bottles of cheap bubbly popped and, after three hearty cheers, we drank a toast from plastic cups.

The ritzy lodge was originally built and operated by the Bush Pilots Airline based in Cairns and later taken over by Ansett Australia. Here, the beer was cold, the grass green and soft, the showers hot, the amenities flushed, mobile phones worked and a classy restaurant opened out into tropical gardens beside the swimming pool. That night we celebrated with dinner in the resort. It felt like heaven. The Honourable Leneen Forde, AC, then Governor of Queensland, was also there that night. Because she was dressed informally, we were unaware of her presence until after dinner. During the meal, one of our passengers accidentally bumped her chair and casually apologised with, 'Sorry, love.'

A ferry from the mainland connected Thursday Island—

thirty-nine kilometres north from the tip of Cape York in the Torres Straight—to the mainland, and most of the group wanted to go. The island's rich history of Melanesian culture, pearl trade, military fort and the Japanese bombing of nearby Horn Island attracted many tourists. We needed an early start to shuttle passengers to the wharf from where the ferry departed, so not wanting to wake the whole campground, I parked the bus outside the camp the night prior, and Lindy served breakfast very quietly. Not all passengers were keen to make the voyage because it was often over rough seas, so, with the correct number of people on the bus, we made a slow, quiet departure. In the rear-view mirrors, I spotted one of our group running right through the middle of the campsite yelling at the top of her voice, 'Bruce, wait for me.' She'd decided at the last minute to catch the bus to the wharf and back, just for the ride.

On the eve of the southbound leg, I noticed the fuel tank repairs done at Lakeland Downs had failed, so I shut it down, leaving us just one workable tank to get home. Based on the northbound trip, my calculations suggested we should get to the next refuelling point at Archer River. We started south on a Sunday morning and found the only fuel station closed. Luckily, back in Seisia, a fisherman with a diesel-powered vessel sold us his only spare forty-four-gallon drum of fuel, and we gratefully transferred it into the bus, but the tank still wasn't full.

I hadn't realised that many passengers could clearly see the fuel gauge, and as the day passed, it sank quickly towards empty and the mood in the bus changed from confidence to impending doom. The red warning light had been on for an hour when we came to a kilometre post showing that Archer River Roadhouse was ten kilometres away. It would take a miracle to make it, but we did. I parked the bus in the campground and left the engine idling for an air supply to inflate the airbeds. As soon as we'd inflated all the mattresses, the engine coughed to a stop—out of fuel.

That same night, as we fumbled around under the poor lighting, somebody filled the billy over the fire with lemon cordial instead of water. Milk curdled instantly in cups of tea made in the dim light, but we were too tired to be bothered by it.

When we reached Mt Carbine, we all enjoyed the wonderful feeling of driving on a bitumen road again—smooth, so smooth.

On the route back home—through western Queensland and outback New South Wales—we stayed in typical country pubs with worn-out sagging mattresses on the beds, bathrooms down the hallway and green-tiled public bars downstairs. The exception was for one night near Tambo, where we booked a farm stay at an attractive tariff and so expected accommodation in the shearers' quarters with very basic meals. We pulled up in front of the grand colonial homestead to ask for directions, and to our surprise and delight, our host showed us to luxurious rooms inside the magnificent building. The rooms all had private bathrooms, and the antique cedar furniture and interior decoration in the style of Laura Ashley highlighted the nineteenth-century rural feel. At dinner time our host ushered us into a formal dining room with a ceiling height of perhaps four metres and wallpapered walls displaying portraits of family ancestors. We sat around a huge cedar dining table for a superb roast dinner served on a willow-patterned dinner set, but better than all this were the grins on our faces. When departing next morning, we paid in cash and were given a discount. I sometimes wonder if it really did happen or whether we were hallucinating after the trials of Cape York.

When eventually back home, Lindy vowed *never* to go back to Cape York. *Not ever!*

But she did—another sixty times.

After several days of cleaning up and resting following that ordeal, Lindy visited the post office and learned from Sue, the proprietor, of a rowdy party held at our place in our absence. We had half expected the boys would do this, so it was no great surprise, but what really dumbfounded us was that she also asked if we enjoyed our holiday.

It was clear to me that Lindy was probably right again. Our machine was not at all suitable for long trips, but word had already spread via those just returned that this really was the trip of a lifetime, and that grew substantial interest for the next time.

~

No way could we afford another bus, and no lender would have taken us on anyway, so we modified what we had. I fitted a bigger engine and overdrive gearbox along with improved seating, and I sent it back to the body builder to have storage bins added. A local coach operator sold us a set of very tidy Pyramid tents, and we built a robust kitchen trailer that gave Lindy what she always wanted—a kitchen with a view. Future trips departed from Cairns, thus cutting out most of the road miles and allowing multiple trips every dry season.

One afternoon, Colton Lamond, a long-time family friend and local dairy farmer, dropped in with an interesting proposal for us. 'Would you consider taking a group of Rotary Exchange students on their annual trek away to Central Australia?'

We jumped at the chance.

Our Rotary district covered the South Coast, Monaro and the ACT, so on the first day of the three-week six thousand kilometres round trip, we collected students at Nowra, Canberra and Yass before going on to Wagga for the first night of camping.

Two Rotarians travelled with us, Phil Broad and Peter Stevens. When we picked up Phil, a prominent Nowra solicitor, in Kangaroo Valley, he was dressed like one of the students with his cap on backwards and Walkman earphones in his ears, and as the trip progressed, he became the life of the party.

The site next to our first camp in Wagga boasted a contingent of military blokes, who understandably noticed the attractive and worldly teenage girls in our group. During the early hours of the morning, we heard some muffled noises coming from the camp kitchen, but we didn't take too much notice until the noise level increased. Eventually, Lindy burst out of our tent to find many of the giggling girls sitting in a tight huddle with the military blokes and sharing cigarettes. She let fly with words far more dangerous than the bullets these blokes might face in battle, and they didn't dare come back near our camp. This episode ensconced her as one not to be messed with, but they quickly learned to love her for the way she looked after them with catering, caring and sometimes even mothering.

Our first scheduled highlight on the trip was a day in the Barossa Valley wine region in South Australia. Our guide for the day was Frank Warnest, a descendant of a pioneering German immigrant and a keen winemaker himself. He took us via the Avenue of Palms—a five kilometre avenue of Canary Island date palms—to the famous Seppeltsfield Winery, where he'd pulled a few strings to get us inside for an inspection. The guide, a nice young bloke, escorted us around the twelve heritage listed bluestone buildings, then took us behind the scenes into the cellars, where he told us of the winery's impressive achievements and success over 130 years. When finished, he asked if there were any questions.

'Yes,' one of the girls said. 'Are you married?'

We realised then where the focus of these kids lay.

From the Barossa Valley, our route took us into Australia's dead heart, over Goyder's Line, beyond which the average annual rainfall was less than ten inches. Our passengers' eyes soon glazed over as they stared out the windows across endless expanses of nothingness. We likely looked the same because this was our first time in the desert too. The outline of Wilpena Pound came into view, rising about eighty kilometres in the distance above the saltbush-covered plains, and the blue-grey-mauve colours of the mountains improved as we approached in the afternoon light. The ring of tall mountains shaped like a cupped hand gave early pioneer graziers a natural enclosure for their flocks and herds. We stayed in a woolshed facility on Oraparinna Station outside the Wilpena Pound and next day hiked to the summit of St Mary's Peak, the tallest mountain at almost four thousand feet high. The strenuous ten-hour return walk involved rock scrambling near the summit and really sorted out some of the kids, especially those who'd never been out of a big city in their lives. That night was the first time everyone went to bed early—we were all exhausted. At 4.00 am I heard heavy rain outside and knew we'd be stranded for days if we didn't make a move to get out right then. That country doesn't soak up water well, and numerous normally dry creeks crossed the road out. Flood waters would quickly make them impassable. We needed to get out ASAP.

We rallied everyone out of bed, loaded the bus and set off along the road. Flood waters had already begun to flow through the many gullies, making driving difficult. As the day broke, we relaxed a little, but rainstorms continued all around us and there could be no turning back. I took a deep breath and headed out onto the Oodnadatta Track from Marree, hoping to reach the old railway town of Oodnadatta 405 kilometres distant that night. Without our knowledge, the road had been closed just minutes after we started out. A large capable off-road vehicle like ours will either get you out of trouble or into way bigger trouble further from help. We slipped and slid our way towards Oodnadatta, driving the timeless route into Central Australia following the string of springs. Aboriginals trading between tribes had used this ancient route for thousands of years, and explorer John McDouall Stuart followed on the first ever return crossing of the continent in 1862. Australia's overland telegraph line went this way in 1872, as did the Ghan Railway and the first road through to Alice Springs in 1929. I pondered the history of that historic route and wondered if there was any other place in the modern world like it. Where else can you walk several kilometres off to the side of a famous, well-used thoroughfare and see a landscape much the same as it has been for millennia?

Finally, the lights of Oodnadatta came into sight, and we hurriedly established camp in the darkness behind the famous Pink Roadhouse. Everyone was tired, and the surrounds weren't at all inspiring, so most retired early. Against the rules requiring an alcohol-free trip, I sneaked away to the pub—but I just needed a beer. When small groups of students randomly appeared at the pub, I sent them back out the door.

Next morning, when the sun rose and we looked around us in the daylight, the lacklustre surroundings didn't look any better. We abandoned the original plan to continue through to Finke via the old Ghan Railway line route and, instead, headed for Marla Bore with its civilisation and sealed roads. From there it was easy driving into the Northern Territory and on to Yulara Resort campground near Uluru—called Ayres Rock until 1993.

The group wanted to climb the rock very early next morning so they could be on the top at sunrise. We'd never been there before, but we eventually found the starting point for the climb by shining headlights towards the rock. Twenty kids exited the bus and charged up the precipitous climb, leaving us well behind. In the haste to keep up, I overlooked applying the park brake. It shouldn't be too much of a problem in dead flat terrain, should it?

We caught up to the group on top and experienced one of nature's greatest light shows. You hear about sights being breathtaking, but this one truly was. Dim eastern lights slowly replaced the darkness, steadily increasing and ever-changing from subtle pinks and mauves to orange as the sun appeared over the horizon and hit the rock, turning it bright red.

On the western side, the ancient Olgas stood silhouetted against the big colourful sky, and we could see to the flat horizon in all directions. Something else we saw from up there came as even more of a surprise. A big yellow 6WD bus sat out in the middle of the road. I hadn't thought the bus rolling away was possible, even with the park brake not applied, but it was, and it did, apparently in very slow motion, because when we got back down to it, rows of pebbles showed where bystanders had attempted to chock the wheels with anything they could find.

Later that day we walked into the Valley of the Winds among the red domes of the Olgas, then drove back to Uluru in time for sunset viewing. We parked the big yellow bus in among several dozen shiny tourist coaches and watched with amazement as people from all over the world enjoyed the extraordinary sight while sipping a glass of champagne and consuming hors d'oeuvres served from tables clad with lace tablecloths. Our group really stood out, especially when I opened the roof hatches and invited all our kids to climb up onto the roof of the bus to better enjoy the sight. We watched in awe as the huge rusty-orange rock that thrust up from the middle of a vast flat plain changed colour to sizzling red and back to orange again.

On that evening I took a stroll around the other coach

groups and learned a lot from listening and watching how those experienced tour operators presented this spectacle. They were good—very good—and we needed to improve hugely if we were to succeed in this coach game. Humour was a common trait, and I overheard a conversation between an American bloke and his coach driver about the microwave communication towers spaced throughout the outback.

'What are all those tower things for?' he asked.

'They're loudspeakers, mate,' the driver said, straight-faced, 'to play music for the cows.'

'Man, I never heard such a thing,' the guy said. 'What sort of music do cows like?'

With absolute authority the driver replied, 'Brahms.' (Brahman cattle are the dominant breed out there.)

The yank wandered away, shaking his head.

Sunset viewing – Rotary trek away at Uluru.

We moved on to Alice Springs and set up camp at the Gapview Resort. This was our first visit to 'the Alice' and we weren't disappointed. Like Uluru, the landscape was particularly beautiful in the soft evening and morning lighting, so we drove the students up onto Anzac hill to enjoy the sunset and orientate ourselves with the town. The bed of the Todd River was dry, and the smoke from many campfires burning along the banks hung low in the stillness of the evening. An occasional note from a didgeridoo echoed up the dry riverbed as we sat quietly absorbing the sights and sounds in the smoky evening.

A large chain-mesh security fence with barbed wire along the top surrounded the campground at the Gapview Resort—not to keep people in, but to keep others out. The Todd River ran near the hotel, so we were in a high foot traffic zone. At night the gates were locked, and we had a key for emergencies, so we slept confidently, knowing our group would be safe for the night. Late at night several kids having a chat in the kitchen near our tent woke Lindy. She investigated and found them rummaging in the first aid box. One of the girls had a bandaged finger and when quizzed replied that she'd burned herself when ironing. We didn't think any more about it, but long after the tour finished, we heard the real story. Three of the kids decided to go to the pub, but when climbing over the barbed wire fence, one girl caught her finger on a barb and tore it deeply. They spent their big night out in casualty having the finger stitched and precautionary injections. Apparently, later in the tour at Broken Hill, they sneaked away again and went to casualty to have the stitches removed.

We learned that you can't judge anyone by their appearance, something we were regularly reminded of over the next thirty plus years. One Japanese girl seemed very quiet and proper and appeared a bit left out of things. But when we took the students to the School of the Air in Broken Hill and the on-air teacher asked if anyone played the piano, the Japanese girl raised her hand. She sat at the keyboard, and at first we thought we were listening to a recording. I felt my hair stand on end because she was simply magnificent. She played some opera, then played and sang the pop song 'Sukiyaki'.

Another lesson on not judging by appearances happened when we visited Simpsons Gap at sunset, and the sun reflected off the mirror-smooth water in the Gap, casting golden light on the ancient palm-fringed canyon walls. This time, another Japanese girl impressed us when, in perfect English, she said, 'It is like the gateway to heaven.'

On the return leg, the Bushy developed a minor problem when an adjuster bracket for the alternator broke. We pulled into a small South Australian town at lunchtime and found a workshop behind a service station. The owner/ mechanic asked the normal questions, like what the tour group was and where we were headed. To my astonishment, after hearing the answers, he started scolding me. He was a Rotarian, and if he'd known we were coming through his town, he would've arranged for his club to welcome us and host the group for lunch. Even though he intended closing the workshop and going home for lunch, he left it open for me and gave me full access to all the tools so I could repair the bus without further delay.

We did several more 'Trekaways' in the years that followed and hosted students ourselves. Hosting was something we really enjoyed doing, and I'm sure our boys did as well. Christa from Portland, Oregon, and Lucy from Sao Paulo, Brazil, each stayed with us for several months. We took them away with us on trips, and they fitted in very well at home.

~

On one trip to Cape York, we were the first large tour vehicle to reach the top after the wet season. Before the bridge was built, the Wenlock River was always the last big obstacle, so several Cairns-based tour operators stationed vehicles north of the Wenlock before the wet season, then transferred passengers over the river by boat. We arrived at the deep crossing point and plunged the big yellow bus into the deep water just as a boat full of passengers from another tour operator started over the river. I don't know how those in the boat felt, but we felt like nothing could stop us as we raced past them at eye level to loud cheering.

Another method existed for getting over the Wenlock—a pontoon raft made from forty-four-gallon drums. In the days before safety management systems, risk assessments, expensive public liability policies and Tripadvisor reviews, some operators risked their vehicles and passengers by crossing the crocodile-infested river on this pontoon.

We only ever took one tour group into the Iron Range National Park on the eastern side of Cape York, but what a trip it was. The Illawarra Bird Observers chartered us to take them into the park, hoping to spot the rare magnificent riflebird, red-bellied pitta and yellow-billed kingfisher.

In the oppressive heat and humidity with no cooling breeze, we set up camp under the closed canopy of the tropical rainforest in Iron Range. Noises from all the rainforest creatures echoed around us and soon became overbearing, especially the sound of the male magnificent rifle bird who perched right above the camp, continually doing his courtship with dancing perch displays. He impressed us, but apparently not his female, because for the whole time we were there, he didn't shut up. Every five minutes or so, he extended his wings fully, raised his tail, then jerked upwards while swinging his head from side to side to expose his metallic blue-green breast shield and yelled 'whoosh' while flapping his wings. To see this for the first time was incredible—but enough is enough. Yellow-billed kingfishers were as common as seagulls and very easy to spot, but to see the red-bellied pitta required twitchers (keen bird watchers) to scramble through the bush on their hands and knees. Soon they broke out with angry red lumps in armpits, pelvic regions and sweat areas—the dreaded scrub itch—caused by brushing mites off the foliage onto their skin. But they seemed fulfilled to add such a rare 'lifer' to their bird list.

Around dinnertime the first night, a park ranger drove in and joined us for a cold drink or six and seemed intent on staying for dinner when he saw Lindy serving corned beef with white mustard sauce and fresh vegetables. He drove away very late after entertaining us with his fascinating stories of life as a ranger and his army experiences in Vietnam. Next morning, he turned up for breakfast and offered to take me out to Chilli Beach to see if the bus could fit along the narrow track. We were away the whole day, cleaning toilets, repainting park directional signs, collecting camp fees and stopping everyone who looked dubious. Drug smugglers often came ashore at isolated places like Iron Range to escape the prying eyes of law enforcement. We were both thirsty after a big day, so again passed the evening with the routine of drinks, dinner and his endless astonishing stories.

Next day, we visited all the sites the ranger suggested. A clear area near Lockhart River showed where a massive blast was set off in 1963. Codenamed 'Operation Blowdown', it simulated the impact of a nuclear blast on tropical rainforest. Thirty years later the forest had still not recovered. We saw abandoned airfields, gun emplacements, roads, bridges and a jetty at Portland Roads and thousands of bullets scattered on the beaches fronting Weymouth Bay left from WWII.

Our dinner guest appeared right on schedule, and afterwards

he confessed his real story. He was Pat Shears, probably the most sought-after person in Queensland at the time because of his key role in the Foxtail Palm Affair, a scandal then raging back in civilisation. Foxtail palms were unknown until 1978 in the outside world beyond a local Aboriginal community in Far North Queensland's remote Cape Melville National Park. Demand for the valuable seeds came from all over the world, bringing seed poachers who caused significant damage by vandalising park gates, trampling undergrowth, felling whole stands of trees, poaching protected wildlife and depleting natural seed banks.

Just a couple of weeks prior, Pat had been a ranger alert for these poachers in Cape Melville National Park. He came across some suspicious tyre tracks running through a smashed park gateway, so investigated on foot using the stealth techniques he learned in the jungles of Vietnam. He found a Toyota Landcruiser loaded with weapons and chainsaws and heard the nearby voices of the suspected poachers. Fearing they were armed, he hijacked the Landcruiser and drove it out of the park, leaving them stranded. One of the stranded poachers was a brother to the premier of Queensland's principal private secretary, and within days, government interference was suspected. A political scandal raged and threats made, so Pat's employer, the Department of Environment and Heritage, sent him into hiding in the Iron Range National Park.

Unknowingly, we were hosting a marked man on the run from ruthless lawbreaking poachers and some very angry individuals in high places.

~

We met many of the pioneers and characters of Cape York because the big yellow bus attracted so much attention. Dallas

Oswald Nixon was one.

After a couple of painstaking hours of driving along the corrugated track just north of Bramwell Station, we stopped for morning tea beside some old cattle yards. We heard a noisy vehicle approaching slowly, its racket due to having a stock crate that rattled over the bumps and no muffler. Eventually an old International cattle truck with the front door missing appeared through the scrub, driven by an old bloke sitting on bare seat springs, so low in the cab he peered through the steering wheel to see where he was going. When the truck stopped near us, a skinny, bare-footed wiry but otherwise tidy bloke slid out and extended his hand to me.

'G'day, mate. Dal's my name. That's Dal, short for Dallas,' he said loudly while raising his worn old scrubber's hat.

'Cup of tea, Dal?' Lindy asked.

'Strong and black, thanks, love,' he replied politely.

Dal talked for an hour about his expansive Shelburne Station that occupied all the country to the east, stretching thirty kilometres to the coast. On several previous trips, we'd noticed a bush track leading off in that direction marked by two rough signs hand-painted on rusty old sheets of corrugated iron. The first read 'Shelburne Station' and the second warned 'Cranky old bastard lives here'!

He told how he and his wife Eileen took up their pastoral lease in 1959 when the only access was on horseback and how, over years of backbreaking work, they managed to make a living on such poor country. First, they built a tin-shed homestead and cut a vehicular track in from the telegraph line with ramped approaches to crocodile-infested creek crossings dug out with pick and shovel. Eventually he bought a bulldozer and 'walked' it two hundred kilometres at six kilometres an hour all the way from the bauxite mines at Weipa.

Dal talked with such a passion for the area that he'd only drunk half his cup of tea by the time we had to get going. We still had a long, slow and challenging drive ahead that day. Our paths never crossed again with Dal, but in the years following, we heard plenty about him.

The poor fellow and his wife 'worked their guts out' on that pastoral lease but became victims of a monumental battle for the property. The world's best resources of vivid-white silica sand sat along the coastal portion of their land in dunes so high and vast they were known as the Snowfields of Shelburne Bay. Added to this were Aboriginal land claims and national parks interest, along with the site being identified as perfect for a commercial spaceport for launching rockets into orbit.

If the Nixons had a lease almost anywhere else in Queensland, it would've likely been routinely renewed, but not at that location. The Channel Nine program '60 Minutes' highlighted their plight, but very sadly Dal suffered a severe stroke brought on by years of stress. He was nursed in Mareeba before passing away and his ashes spread at the cattle yards right where we shared that cuppa with him. A simple plaque is there today.

On one of our many trips up to Cape York, we met Noel Pearson, one of Australia's best-known advocates for Aboriginal people, when we stopped at the Palmer River Roadhouse south of Cooktown for a quick break. Even though our meeting was brief, it was long enough to recognise the quality of the man and his genuine interest in the people of the Cape.

We met the controversial author Rodney Liddell many times. One of his books, *The Savage Frontier*, promoted a history of Cape York that some disagreed with to the point where he was banned from ever going north of the Jardine River again. He met our groups at the campground in Weipa and, after a short talk, sold signed copies of his book. His second book, *Children of Destiny*, told his incredible story of being one of the eighty-six babies from unwed mothers to American soldiers born during the war and raised at the Hopewood Home in Bowral.

Mal Coventry of Cooktown Tours was an amusing character we always engaged to guide our groups around Cooktown. Mal came from an era before political correctness, but we all forgave him because he was amusingly offensive to everyone. He delighted in showing us Cooktown's West Coast Hotel on the east coast, the drinking water fountain dedicated to a person who perished from thirst, the grave of a sailor who died at sea named Albert Ross (albatross) and many Chinese graves from the gold rush era.

When touring on Cape York we enjoyed an occasional night in 'luxury' at the Hillcrest Guest House in Cooktown. The owner/host, Verna, a sophisticated woman from the city, had just bought the guesthouse when we stayed for the first time. She welcomed us beautifully wearing a designer dress, heels and makeup, but after a couple of years, she adapted to Cooktown to the point where she met us in T-shirt, bike shorts and bare feet. Her style showed in the way she decorated the old guesthouse into quite a classy place, and guests often expressed their compliments. A real character with a brilliant sense of humour, she did whatever it took to accommodate our groups, even if it meant moving out of her own quarters and sleeping in the office to gain an extra room.

One night while sleeping in the office, at around 4:00 am, she remembered she hadn't turned something off in the kitchen. With nobody around she took the risk of not getting dressed and sneaked out to the kitchen just as a breeze blew the office door shut and locked behind her. What was she to do? Thinking quickly, she wrapped a tablecloth around herself like a sarong and just went to work early. At breakfast, guests were amazed with her attention to detail even to the point of dressing to match the tablecloths.

Verna took time to settle in at Cooktown and often phoned her son at the fire station not always knowing if he was on duty. After a few weeks, she read an article in the local newspaper about an inconsiderate pest who kept setting off the fire station siren during the night. No one had told her that if the station was unmanned, any unanswered calls set off the siren.

~

That big yellow bus was also one of the first tour vehicles able to travel to Cobbold Gorge near Forsayth, Queensland. At the time Simon Terry was diversifying his huge cattle station into tourism and hadn't yet acquired his own 4WD shuttle buses to take sightseers from his campgrounds down the rough track to the gorge. Cobbold Gorge tourism has since grown to be one of the Gulf's best attractions.

While the bus had its advantages, it also caused some issues. One night we had a bush camp on Black Braes Station between the Lynd Junction and Hughenden in Queensland. We were all sitting snugly around the campfire after dinner and noticed one lady quietly stand up and leave the gathering. We had no toilets that night, so she thought she'd take the opportunity for some privacy to 'go bush', knowing everybody else was beside the fire. Problem was that she went around the far side of the bus and overlooked completely that the machine was very high off the ground. She was way too exposed.

Another time we accepted our first charters from the Kiama Travel Club and took a group from Cairns to Darwin around the Gulf and brought another back to Cairns. Our season had gone very well, and as we started the three-day 'deadhead' (without passengers) drive back home, I remarked to Lindy how good it felt to finally have a small credit balance in the bank.

After a full day of driving, we refuelled with bad fuel, and the engine started blowing smoke and became difficult to start. I hoped to get it home and nursed it along as best I could. At night I parked where next morning it could roll away for a clutch start, but we only got to Marlborough, about one hour north of Rockhampton, where we stopped for dinner at a roadhouse. Afterwards, the engine just wouldn't start, so I managed to jump the crippled machine on the starter motor around the back of the roadhouse and phoned Cummins in Rockhampton for help.

They sent a mobile mechanic who arrived early next day with a new injector pump. Not a massive job to changeover if the vehicle had a tilt cab, but ours was in a very confined space. The mechanic, although very capable, dropped the shaft key into the timing-gear case so then the radiator had to be removed and the front of the engine opened to retrieve the key.

For three days we lived on roadhouse food and managed to pick up a distant radio signal by turning a steel washstand into an AM aerial. While stranded there, we worked hard cleaning up all the camp gear and tents so that there would be one less job to do before the next tour.

Repairs cost us roughly what we had in the bank.

The big yellow 6WD bus did several hundred thousand kilometres in our service over those early years and left us with some great memories. An operator near Port Stephens bought it from us and put it to work in the harsh, salty and abrasive environment of Stockton Beach for another fifteen years.

We often thought about it and knew where it was, but this didn't help to ease the deep regret I felt for selling it in the first place. That bus established us in the bus business and was central to so many of our fond memories.

Maybe it was a bad idea, but recently we drove to Port Stephens with the intention of buying it back to restore for nostalgic reasons. What we found was just a sad rusting hulk sitting out in a paddock with blackberries growing all through it.

I feel hollow whenever I think about it.

3
We're Going to Need a Bigger Bus

L ike most bus operators back in the early 1990s, I subscribed to several industry magazines such as *Truck and Bus* and the *Australasian Bus and Coach* magazines. Each issue had classified advertisements for used equipment that I scoured hoping to find a replacement for the Bushmobile but, of course, we never did. Occasionally, someone advertised larger 4WD coaches, but they always sold quickly. After a while I realised the only way to get one was to buy a conventional host vehicle and convert it to 4WD.

Eventually, a suitable machine for conversion came up for sale in Melbourne. It sounded ideal with the engine up the front, a walk-in luggage compartment at the back, good bins underneath and most importantly, a robust Australian-built Austral Domino body.

At the time we were flat out with touring and had just one day free to inspect it. We set off from Bomaderry at two in the morning in Lindy's little Peugeot 505 and arrived in Melbourne 840 kilometres away around midday. The bus was ideal, so we bought it and arranged to pick it up later, then headed straight back up the Hume Highway towards home.

Around nightfall a highway patrol officer pulled me over because I hadn't dipped the headlights when entering Bookham. Bookham was appropriately named since truckies feared it for being the favourite hunting ground for the New South Wales Police Highway Patrol. He rightfully suspected I was tired and asked where we'd driven from. My answer was sort of true— Melbourne. He spotted my driver's logbook on the back seat and, knowing I was a professional driver, gave me a lecture, saying I should know better. Lindy took his side, telling him she was unhappy with me too because I just wouldn't stop for a rest. Eventually he let me off with a warning, knowing Lindy would enforce a rest stop in Yass. Her skilful diplomacy saved me again, but I wonder what he would've done had he known the full story.

After bringing the 'new' bus home, a six-month conversion project started. RFW in Chester Hill did the conversion to 4WD and fitted the rear air suspension. A mate, Trevor Mackie, installed a brand-new Cummins C-8.3 engine along with a nine-speed overdrive Road Ranger transmission. The exterior was re-painted, the sliding windows replaced with fixed tinted glass, a Thermoking 'flying suitcase' air conditioner installed on the roof and the interior re-trimmed.

We reduced the adventure component of all our tours to match the lesser off-road capacity of the longer bus. Several regular passengers then admitted to me that they knew of many folks who'd been scared away by the extreme adventures we'd been doing with the big yellow bus.

This bus could carry forty passengers plus driver and hostess, almost double that of the big yellow bus. Profitability improved quickly, and finally we began to make a quid.

It's funny how sometimes the simplest suggestion can turn fortunes around. Someone suggested we should advertise in the monthly Probus News magazine circulated to all Probus members, who were mostly retired professional or business people seeking social connection through activities like group travel. How pleased we were to have the bigger bus when tours started selling briskly.

Working with people of our parents' generation fitted perfectly with us, so we let go of the school and backpacker promotions and closed the hostel. The big building became our home and main-street office, and the carpark proved handy for bus and customer car parking.

Around this time my old mate Bruno, after working for six years in the Snowy Mountains, returned to the district with his now wife, Christine, and their growing family. He'd worked his way up the ladder to being manager of guest relations at the new Thredbo Visitors' Information Centre and had almost completed a course in travel and tourism. His ultimate employment ambition was to join TAFE (Technical and Further Education), so while waiting for the opportunity, he volunteered to help Lindy computerise the office to better cope with the increased activity. Halfway through the job, his opportunity came up with TAFE, and we were pleased to see him progress. Christine took over the task, using knowledge gained when managing holiday lettings for L J Hooker in Jindabyne. She came for several weeks but stayed for several decades.

~

Restoration and conversion of the bus was a huge job, and the first booking we had was for a Rotary 'Trekaway' to Central Australia. The bus wasn't ready in time, so we chartered a coach and driver from Gerringong Coaches. Lindy went away on tour without me while I stayed at home to finish the job, run the hostel and try to manage our three boys. This was a lot harder than I'd anticipated because they were now in their late teens and had become very independent due to our many periods away. Had it not been for Lindy's big sister, Jan, we would've starved, because I'd never attempted to run a household before. I learned very quickly to only stock the fridge with unpopular brands of beer so the boys and their hairy-legged mates wouldn't drink it all—and I still do.

Lindy arrived back after three weeks away, leaving just three days to 'deadhead' the new bus to Cairns, 2,700 kilometres away. I drove the maximum hours allowed, which meant driving right through the night to keep on schedule. After going through Rockhampton at sunrise, and feeling a little tired after an all-nighter, we stopped at traffic lights behind a tradie's ute and noticed him rolling slowly backwards. I gave him a blast on the air horn just as he hit our bulbar. He took off like a rocket. Oops, it was us rolling forward, not him rolling backwards.

The first tour to Cape York in the bigger bus was the most challenging trip we'd ever attempted due to the late wet season. All went well as far as the Wenlock River, where the water was so deep, we pushed a bow wave which almost lapped up to the windscreen. Bigger problems lay ahead just north of the turn-off to Eliot Falls, where we found massive erosion to the track and a deep gully where the track once was for as far as we could see ahead. Off to the western side, some wheel tracks ran into the bush, threading around the larger trees. A group of Toyota drivers were ahead of us, and they'd obviously detoured here, but the path they took was much too narrow to squeeze the big bus through. I walked around the washed-out stretch for several kilometres and picked the most feasible detour path, then with a chainsaw, and many willing helpers, cut a bypass track. After a big day of exhausting effort, we made it to the Jardine River Ferry by nightfall. What should've taken a couple of hours to travel took all day.

Impassable road after wet season floods.
Cape York, Queensland, 1997.

For the rest of that dry season, all the traffic followed our track, and many years later, when the new gravel road was constructed, it followed the path we cut.

Driving that bus took some time to master, because the driver's seat was well forward of the steer axle. On the highway it made no difference, but tight situations were a horse of a different colour. I found the biggest challenge driving the road to the Wombeyan caves, where negotiating tight corners required using all the available road space. I never adjusted to sitting out over the cliff edge when making those sharp outside lefthand turns.

~

On a Cape York tour, heading south out of Bamaga, rain started falling just when we reached the Jardine River Ferry. Normally, Jacob, a very capable old Aboriginal bloke, skippered it and, being very shy, just gave hand signals to drivers. Lindy always gave him lunch and replaced his Bishops cap whenever it looked shabby. But on this day, a new skipper was on duty, and everybody remained in the bus due to the heavy rainstorm. The ferry operation was something like might be found in a Third World country, and carrying a heavy bus pushed it beyond its limits. Getting the bus on without dragging the rear and ripping up decking boards required the skipper to beach the vessel higher up the ramp to reduce the approach angle. With a sixteen-ton bus onboard, the ferry couldn't pull itself off the ramp, so I accelerated forward and slammed on the brakes to jar it off the ramp. When underway, I reversed as far as I dared to lift the front enough to improve the egress angle.

Without us noticing, a small truck followed the bus onto the ferry and parked right up close behind where it couldn't be seen, and the new skipper either didn't see him or didn't understand the normal procedure. We performed the routine manoeuvre and drove off as usual, but a little truck with a smashed-in front soon overtook us and broadsided across the road, blocking our path. The furious driver launched himself out of the truck and went into an uncontrolled rage by running around the bus, punching the sides and shouting that we had tried to kill him. We were speechless. His rage even shocked the passengers on board, but eventually we calmed him down enough to stop him harming any of us or himself.

Apparently, as we'd reversed on the ferry to raise the front, we almost pushed that poor bloke and his truck off the back into the crocodile-infested river. At this very spot, just a few weeks prior, a saltwater crocodile had killed a person swimming tools out to the broken-down ferry. The irate driver must've been desperate as we pushed him backwards because two very noticeable rubber skid marks left by his locked brakes marked the deck for years.

Another time we were driving through the heathlands near the Edmund Kennedy monument and saw a cloud of dust coming towards us at high speed. I could do nothing other than pull off the track as far as possible and wait for the approaching vehicle to slam into us. The vehicle broadsided around the blind corner, impacted the bus right on the front wheel hub and deflected away. The impact only slightly damaged the bus, but it destroyed the 4WD ute. Forty very loyal passengers, especially all the irate grandmothers, dealt formidably with the aggressive young driver.

When deadheading for home at the end of a busy season, we stopped in the little Riverina town of Stockinbingal on a Saturday afternoon for a coffee break, but when we tried to leave, the bus had dead batteries. The bus had two large six-volt batteries joined together in series to give twelve volts, but the only garage in town didn't have any. The mechanic suggested we call a garage in Cootamundra and, yes, they had six-volt batteries in stock. I left Lindy to mind the bus and hitchhiked twenty-five kilometres, intending to catch a taxi back with the heavy batteries. Finally, after sharing the front seat of an old Toyota farm ute with a very friendly red kelpie, I got into Cootamundra and introduced myself to the young attendant working behind the fuel pump console.

'I'm the bloke who phoned you an hour ago about the six-volt batteries,' I said. 'Can I have two, please?'

She pointed to a near-full box of six-volt torch batteries, and in her most pleasant voice said, 'You can have as many as you like. We have plenty.'

I didn't know whether to laugh or cry.

Back at the bus, I managed to stop a farmer passing through town in an old Bedford farm truck and asked him for a tow start. With his help we got back on the road and set a cracking pace for home. Even without any electrical power, we would be fine so long as we didn't turn off the engine. By the time we got to the truck-checking station at Marulan, it was getting dark, but, astonishingly, they let us through with no lights on. When we reached the steep descent into Kangaroo Valley, we were driving by moonlight and with no electrical power to work the engine brake. After driving the mountainous road at walking speed, we eventually made it home.

Being home after each season took a few days to adapt back to normality, and we commented to each other on things like, 'I hadn't remembered this room being so big,' or 'Lindy, do you remember how to work the remote control?' On average during the year, we were home just one night in four with a lot of catching up to do with family and friends.

My father, Colin, was always interested in what we did but only ever came on tour with us once, to Fraser Island. He had a wonderful time, so I invited him to come to Cape York. His answer totally changed our business direction. He said he dearly wanted to, but he couldn't sleep on the ground on an air mattress. I asked why, and he said he wouldn't be able to get up off the ground. If the toughest, most physically resilient man I'd ever known couldn't get up off the ground, then who else couldn't? I asked around and it seemed that most people his age couldn't.

This was such a surprise that we asked him what else we should know. He couldn't get up off a camp stool easily, a wee walk at night was necessary and dietary needs were important.

I had an epiphany!

The conversation gave me the inspiration that led us to develop the 'Bush Lodge' mobile camp.

Three game-changing things had set us on a course and given us the points of difference most businesses strive for. Discovering Yerranderie helped steer us into outback touring, effective advertising in Probus News enticed customers and the Bush Lodge gave retirees the confidence to book tours they never would've dared before.

The Bush Lodge evolved over a couple of seasons and eventually featured large cabin tents with internal lights, a dining marquee with tables and comfortable director chairs, good lighting, flushing toilets and hot showers, very comfortable fold-up beds, a silenced generator providing 240-volt power for recharging phones, shavers, toothbrushes, sleep apnoea machines and so on, as well as a galley with large fridges, freezers, cooktops, cool room, a large 4WD support truck to carry all the equipment, and a two-man team to set up, pack away, load luggage and assist with duties around the camp.

We ran *Probus News* advertisements titled, 'Have you ever wanted to go to Cape York but thought it may be too challenging?'

The phone went berserk!

The Bush Lodge camp was an immediate hit with our passengers, and over the years we often heard many of them proudly talking about how their mates down at the Bowling Club told them that there was no way a silly old bugger like you could ever go to Cape York.

Just a few years before, I'd dreaded camping beside tour-market leaders AAT Kings because of their superior equipment, but now I loved it. I often saw our passengers handing out brochures to other tour groups and boasting about how good the Bush Lodge was and the bargain price they paid. Our passengers became our best promoters.

Bush Lodge camp.

From an operational perspective, the biggest job was erecting and packing away the cabin tents. Initially, our set-up crew carried each tent to its site, unrolled it, assembled the support bars and fed them into the canvas pockets, pegged the corners and then lifted the tent up—a huge job for the crew, especially in the heat of the tropics. Often, we'd arrive at camp in the afternoon to find the crew in a lather of perspiration trying to get set up ready for the group's arrival. On one long, hot day, we travelled south from the tip of Cape York to Archer River and were stunned with what the crew had erected for us that night. Apparently, they made good time so decided to have some fun with the group. They'd arranged all twenty-four cabin tents in a large circle with our tent right in the middle and hammered two tent poles into the ground for makeshift flag poles, which flew Fort Bishop flags at the entrance. The crew, Barry and Judy, stood to attention and saluted us as we got off the bus.

As funny as it was, the tents were much too close to each other to make for a comfortable night's stay. Canvas walls don't insulate the noises of the night, so we had to quickly spread them apart. We dropped them to the ground, removed the corner pegs, left the frames in place and with one person on each corner, simply carried them to the new position. It took just a couple of minutes to shift each tent. That night I thought about how easy the move had been and came up with the system of attaching each tent to an aluminium base frame and folding the canvas with tent frames in place. No more unfolding, fitting frames into the canvas pockets and no more corner pegs. This slashed set-up and pack-up times from two hours to only thirty minutes, and spectators often gathered to watch how quickly and easily the crew did the job. The only real problem with the new system was that tents could blow away in heavy wind before we placed luggage and other items inside to weigh them down. On very windy days, the crew placed them in position but left them flat on the ground until the bus arrived.

One afternoon at Karumba on the shores of the Gulf of Carpentaria exposed the weakness of the system. As we approached the camp, we saw a crowd of people looking up into a tree at a fully erected tent suspended high in the branches.

Apparently, it had been dead calm during set-up, but a rogue whirlwind hit without any warning.

~

To meet the demand the following season, we struck a deal with Cairns-based Coral Coaches to shuttle our groups between Cairns and Weipa so we could keep our 4WD bus north of there in the more difficult conditions. It worked very well, because we drew on their local knowledge and contacts for workshops and suppliers and fitted extra tours into the season.

We experimented with two marketing ideas. We offered groups a free seat for each ten booked and enclosed two promotional booklets in each envelope for mass mailouts with a request that the extra one be given to a neighbour or friend.

Groups of friends as well as larger groups such as birdwatchers, Probus groups, social groups and so on booked tours with us.

A bloke who looked very familiar travelled on one of these tours, and trying to recall where I knew him from tormented me. It later hit me like a sledgehammer. The man was Kevin McGregor, a former rugby referee in Illawarra, the same whistle-happy 'milk bottle' who gave me hell when I'd played. Rugby front rowers never forget stuff, and in the heat of battle, many occasionally said, 'You wait, you bastard,' only to laugh about it later between combatants over a few beers. My delightful task now was to even-up the score.

It wasn't going to be easy, but I had the element of surprise because he hadn't yet remembered me. Kev was a renowned solicitor in Wollongong, so I had to be cautious not to go too far with it. I noted his tent number and asked the crew to place it in the worst possible location in future with the doorway up against a tree so green ants would surely find their way in. If there was a hill, I asked them to make sure they put Kev's tent on the most sloping part and put his bed in the tent with the legs positioned where they might collapse. My great regret when doing this was for Kev's wife, Fae, who would, by association, be collateral damage.

Fae and Kevin.

After several days, Kev remembered where he knew me from and realised why he was getting such a raw deal. He confronted me, then extended his hand in surrender and acknowledged that he'd been 'got'. We both doubled over laughing. Lindy was appalled at me for what I'd done but eventually saw the funny side. Kev and Fae became very close friends and travelled with us dozens more times. For years they were our regular house sitters and even had a photo of our dog stuck on their fridge.

Imagine that—the referee and the hooker being mates.

~

As the business evolved, so did we. I ran the machinery, planned tour itineraries, oversaw the support crew and researched and delivered tour commentaries, while Lindy kept everyone fed and cared for and ran the office. But with the bigger bus, her task doubled because she now had forty passengers plus a crew of six to feed and look after. It was a huge task, but she thrived when given the challenge. Every morning she bounded out of bed at six to get everyone fed, packed up and onto the bus by eight. When we stopped for morning teas and lunches, she was always first off the bus to get everything ready quickly so that passengers could make the most of their time. At the end of each day, when the rest of us relaxed with a cold drink, she went straight back to work—like the Duracell bunny laying out predinner nibbles—preparing meals and lunches for the following day, before then cleaning away all the mess. By 10 pm, after a quick shower, she'd slump into bed and be asleep as soon as her head hit the pillow.

If we had a couple of days between tours, she often pushed six trolleys of supplies out of the supermarket, then wrapped, refilled, froze, rotated and packed all this into the support-truck kitchen. When the wholesalers delivered supplies, she had to carefully stow them away as well. She rubbed and scrubbed everything and did the laundry, and when she'd done all that, out came the laptop to pay wages and business accounts. However, she spoke to the boys on the phone as if she had all the time in the world and they were her only interest.

I once asked her why she was so meticulous doing the big clean-ups, and she said she wanted all the equipment to look like brand new, so each passenger thought they were the first to use it. Her capacity to cope with this assiduous workload for months, years and decades on end without becoming tired and snappy was impressive, but to do it in good humour and always flashing that lovely big smile was astonishing.

~

One Probus Club group we took to Cape York became known as 'the tour from hell'! They came from a very wealthy part of Melbourne, and I guess many people in the group were on the tour because everybody else was, and they didn't really know what to expect. As they travelled up the Peninsula Development Road with Coral Coaches, our satellite phone started to ring.

First, Mary from Musgrave Station rang to warn us after they stayed for the night. 'Lindy, you poor thing, you have the tour from hell coming to join you.' She told us they complained about everything: the barman served drinks in the wrong glasses, and they hadn't been chilled; the waitress placed meals from the wrong side; there was no table service from the bar; the wine list was inadequate and so on. They dressed formally for dinner with the men in coats and ties and the ladies wearing heels and jewellery.

Next, Sherrill from the Archer River Roadhouse called with a similar warning, so we braced ourselves for what lay ahead. Mary and Sherrill were correct, it was indeed the tour from hell. We met them as planned in Weipa, where the southbound group swapped buses with the northbound group. We farewelled possibly the best group we'd ever had and replaced them with the worst.

Before we even had a chance to introduce ourselves, they gave a barrage of requests and demands, like wanting a particular brand of cornflakes and how to get ice cubes for a makeshift ice bucket in camp.

One lady insisted on having her special type of hot milk before bed each night to which Lindy said she would try. 'Look dear, it's no big deal,' the woman told Lindy gruffly, 'just put it in the microwave for thirty seconds.'

What microwave?

They became worse and harder to deal with as the days passed until the situation came to a head when one of the group leaders growled rudely at me about something else he thought was wrong. I'd reached my breaking point. After cooling off a bit, I grabbed a couple of camp chairs and cold beers and asked him to join me for a chat. I wanted to understand his behaviour and, if possible, gain his confidence, so I took him well away from the group where we could sit privately for a frank talk, man to man, over a beer. Over the years our confidence grew in the way we managed each tour based on plenty of trial and error and making changes based on valid feedback from past travellers. I knew our product was good and that most passengers enjoyed the way we looked after them, so I was disappointed and dismayed to have unhappy passengers. The complexity of human behaviour has always baffled me, so I mostly left these situations for Lindy to deal with using her natural gift of diplomacy and genuine Christian care for all people.

Anyway, this time, for some obscure reason, I stupidly took it upon myself to sort out the issues using my experience gained in disputes with truck drivers, labourers, truck mechanics and rugby front rowers. What always worked for me was to call them a dopey bastard, joke about knocking their blocks off and then talk it out over a beer.

I took him quietly aside, handed him a beer and calmly asked that he not talk to me like that again.

'I am seventy-five years old, and I will talk to you in any way

I wish!' he replied bluntly.

I nodded. 'I understand that and assure you of our commitment to making your tour a happy one, but please, it's not helpful to be spoken to like that.'

His reply was something along the lines that I should go forth and multiply.

I felt the blood rush to my head and apologised to him that I was not being clear enough. 'Let me put it to you another way that might be a little less obscure,' I said. 'If you ever speak to me like that again, I will put you off the tour.'

'You can't do that.'

'Yes, I can, and I will—check the fine print on your ticket.'

He stormed off, leaving me sitting there on my own. *That went well,* I thought to myself.

To my absolute amazement, with the ringleader silenced, the attitude and mood of the tour changed completely within a couple of days, and everyone started to settle down. Several people in the group individually took me aside to apologise for the rudeness of some. The tour from hell ended quite happily with some even saying it was the best one they ever did. We dropped them back to their five-star hotel in Palm Cove, and I wonder if they heard our loud 'Woohoo' as we drove away.

~

Lindy and I lived in two separate worlds during those frantic years. Our personal lives with family and friends at home, and our professional lives when away on tour. If someone from our personal life came on tour, it really threw us out of whack, but we loved it too. One such time was when our neighbours and good friends John and Carol, joined by Lordy, a former rugby teammate, travelled with us to Cape York. They were also good mates.

John and Carol became great friends after they moved from Victoria and bought the neighbouring property to ours separated by a canal. Before first meeting them, our golden Labrador dog came home wringing wet with a polite note tied around her collar saying, 'I am a naughty girl. I swam the canal and ate all your new neighbour's cat food.' So over we went to apologise, make ourselves known and welcome them. This started a wonderful friendship that continues today even between our children and grandchildren. It would've been so different had they shot the dog.

Usually, early in each tour, I gave a talk about what to expect, particularly about what a challenge it was keeping the machinery running with it being bashed every day in such harsh conditions. I explained my nightly routine of getting under the bus to check, adjust, tighten, grease and so on. Often, as I worked away at night, passengers held me up and sometimes even annoyed me, especially if I was tired and dealing with a problem. Maybe I sounded a bit like Basil Fawlty as time passed, because I introduced an exclusion zone of twenty-five metres around the toolbox that the wives of those needing to tell me how to do my job enforced for me. I promised to give information about bus issues on a need-to-know basis. That is, if you need to know, I will tell you. Having just finished my intolerant talk from the driver's seat, I noticed a big problem behind that required an immediate U-turn. I had no choice other than to announce, 'Well, you need to know this … the trailer is missing.'

We retraced our route for several kilometres and were very relieved to see it sitting undamaged beside the track. The towbar on the bus had broken and needed welding, so I decided to leave the trailer where it was, drive on for an hour to where camp had been set up for the night and return with the support truck.

Lordy and John volunteered to sit with the trailer and guard it until I returned. Three hours later I arrived back to find quite a situation. Instead of guarding the trailer, they'd ransacked it. They had found and drunk Lindy's cooking sherry and eaten that night's sponge-cake dessert and were in no real shape to help me hitch the trailer. Then I had to suffer their humour all the way to the camp.

Having people from our private life travelling with us was always very special, particularly our boys. All three of them said how much fun it was to travel with mostly retired people who sought enjoyment in nearly all situations. It was for us too. Joe came with us on one of our trips into the Bungle Bungles. We camped beside a group of backpackers and found it hard not to notice the pretty girls. Joe commented that it was a shame we didn't have passengers like that on our tour. One of the old blokes butted in, saying they probably were, but he was fifty years too late.

Retired-age folk, however, created one big issue in camp— snoring. Tents are not great for absorbing noises, so the only solution was to spread them apart. As each tour progressed, the crew updated their 'list of shame' of those whose tents needed to be further away, and they often received intelligence anonymously. Sometimes tents could be one hundred metres away, and those banished often didn't realise they had a problem, especially if they were also hard of hearing. Big Brian, a very large man with a hearing aid, caused us even more embarrassing issues. He had wind problems during the night, exaggerated by copious consumption of home brew that he brought with him in four large plastic crates. We moved his tent into the boondocks, and everyone was happy and saw the funny side.

Some months after finishing the tour with big Brian, I was on office duty while Lindy and Christine attended an instructional course on a new business tool called the internet. The phone rang.

'Good morning, Bishops Australian Adventures, Bruce speaking,' I answered.

Bruno had told me to answer all calls this way, and he sometimes phoned if he knew I was on duty, just to test that I was doing it properly. Bruno led the Aussie Host program for TAFE among other initiatives for local businesses to help prepare us for the fast-approaching Sydney Olympic year, and phone-answering procedures were part of it.

The caller said, 'Hello, Bruce, it's big Brian here. Do you remember me?' Or that's what I thought he said because I was using a cordless phone in the workshop, and the noisy air compressor cut in just as he spoke.

'Mate, how could I ever forget you—the most flatulent bugger that ever travelled with us!'

To my great surprise, the caller hung up, so I went into the office, looked up big Brian's number and phoned him back. To my horror, he wasn't the caller.

Hearing what was happening through the night wasn't always a bad thing, though, and for this reason Peter and Shirley from Kiama were useful. Both were quite hard at hearing and spoke too loudly, even at night.

'What time is it, Shirl?'

'Three o'clock, Pete.' And we would all know the time.

Somebody on the bus always had your measure in any circumstance. As we drove into Elliot Falls one time, a young couple walked out of the bush just as I was talking about some of the bird species on the Cape.

I said, 'There is the male and female of the species—the female better known as a double-breasted back-chat.'

Quick as a flash, a sharp-witted lady sitting behind replied,

'And the male is better known as a yellow-bellied sap sucker.' She had my measure and then some.

The routine when southbound from Cape York was to camp beside the Archer River and treat the group to dinner at the roadhouse. Sherrill spoiled us with massive 'Archer River Burgers' served in the beer garden, where we watched the comings and goings of travellers, cattle station workers and truckies heading for the mining town of Weipa.

It was always fun except on State of Origin nights for the thrice-yearly, televised, bloodbath rugby league games between the New South Wales Cockroaches and Queensland Cane toads. The Queensland hosts delighted in seating us under giant posters of Queensland rugby league greats Wally Lewis and Alfie bloody Langer, and we kept a low profile, except if New South Wales won. Any Victorians just sat there like aliens looking bewildered with all the banter.

On one occasion, a ringer gored badly by a wild bush bull that afternoon was driven in from an outlying cattle station, assisted to a seat by his mates and given a cold XXXX beer. His shirt dripped with blood, his face was swollen and bruised, and his ribs apparently broken. Just at kick-off time, a nursing sister arrived from Coen several hours' drive away to attend to his injuries, but the ringer refused any sedation until after the game, so the nurse just stitched him up right there in front of the TV.

Another time (not a State of Origin night), Sherrill seated us in the roadhouse dining room because it wasn't pleasant outside, and we noticed a young woman come in wearing jeans wet to above her knees. The whole group tuned into the conversation between this German traveller and Sherrill.

In broken English, she said, 'The car is in the river.'

Sherrill asked, 'How the heck did you do that?'

The answer was a puzzled, 'Yes.'

With this we noticed Sherrill starting to giggle, and the more she tried to be courteous and understanding, the worse she got. We couldn't contain ourselves either and within seconds the whole place was in uncontrolled laughter, including the poor wet traveller.

Crossing Broken Axle Creek on the track to the top of Cape York, Queensland.

One routine we introduced on long bus days was to invite people to tell us their life stories. What some folk achieved, endured, experienced, suffered, rejoiced in and committed to in their lives was amazing. Generally, our passengers were from our parents' generation and had lived through hard times like the

Great Depression and WWII. They struggled in difficult times and, therefore, appreciated the good times. These contributors to Australia accepted and dealt with whatever life threw at them and did so honestly and honourably. So much of their wisdom and attitude to life influenced us, and it was a privilege having them on board.

We listened with intrigue to people such as the retired British Army Colonel who knew Muammar Gaddafi, a senior public servant who stood on the steps of parliament when Gough made his famous speech after being sacked by the Governor General, a huge-framed man who played football alongside Norm Provan, many who had OAMs (Order of Australia Medals), artists, writers, business people and even an eighty-six-year-old great-grandmother with twenty great grandchildren.

Often the act of passing the microphone around in the bus and hearing all the life stories uncovered some incredible coincidences. Like the time a younger lady told of her childhood in a tiny outback town and her favourite first schoolteacher, and the teacher was on the bus. They hadn't recognised each other after so many years. Another story reconnected Lindy's parents with a long-lost friend. On many occasions people shared interests and had connections in common.

One of the most amazing stories we ever heard was from an old bloke telling us why he was travelling with us to Albany, Western Australia. He wanted to see the place where his father was killed when returning by ship from WWI in Europe. Apparently, he went ashore at Albany and arrived back late just as the gangplank was being withdrawn. He tried to leap aboard, but, tragically, he fell and became jammed between the wharf and the ship as it manoeuvred to release the tie ropes. We took him to the site of the accident at the wharf and shared a very emotional time with our elderly passenger. Incredibly, next morning Albany's local newspaper featured the story of this tragic event that happened exactly ninety years before on the front page, and we all felt a little spooked by the coincidence.

Bob Green also told us his remarkable life story. He'd urged his church to install facilities for people with a disability and took on responsibility for the project. For several years he fundraised and supervised the installation of equipment and building upgrades. Just after completion, he suffered a terrible stroke that made him dependent on a wheelchair, so he was the first person to use the new facilities. Bob and Yvonne travelled with us before and after Bob's stroke, and we even hosted them on a tour through the USA many years later.

One night at dinner, Bob said to me, 'We put it over those transport inspectors today, didn't we?'

I was unsure what he meant, but earlier that day several inspectors intent on finding something wrong with the paperwork, vehicle roadworthiness or driver had pulled us over. 'How do you mean, mate?' I asked.

'Well, they checked everything other than the air pressure in the tyres of my wheelchair.' He laughed. 'And look at this; one of them is half flat.'

We listened to many stories of military service, but the best was from Peter Jensen, who flew coastal patrols with the RAF during WWII. In one battle, six German Junkers JU88s attacked and shot down his Sunderland flying boat, and with three engines out, he set down on the Bay of Biscay on a fifteen-foot swell. The crew scrambled out onto the wing and then jumped into the water as one of the German aircraft dived threateningly back towards them. Amazingly, they fired no shots. After twenty-four hours adrift in a raft, the Royal Navy rescued them. Many years later, Peter met one of the German pilots and asked why he hadn't fired at them. He replied that he had—but with a Leica

35 mm camera. Peter sent me a copy of the photos along with the following letter. They've been on my desk ever since.

>*12/8/2008*
>*Dear Bruce,*
>*Enclosed are copies of the photos I promised. Please bear in mind that the shots of us in the drink were taken by the leader of the six JU88s (Heinz Hommel) with a small handheld camera through the Perspex canopy—and he was flying the aircraft at the same time! So they are not very detailed.*
>*I can't remember what I told you about the events, but the first one is when we sank U-boat U461 on the 30th July 1943 and our aircraft was U of 461 Squadron, a coincidence that gets mentioned in every book on the U-boat war. We first attacked a pack of three U-boats on the surface. We sank one (U461), a Halifax sank U462, and the Navy U503. We met another on the way home; his shooting was better than the others and he got us before we got him. We managed to get back to the base but poor old 'U' was so badly damaged it was beyond repair, so we picked up a new aircraft 'E'.*
>*On the 16th September 1943, we were attacked by six JU88s of V Gruppe / Kampfgeschwader 40. Combat lasted nearly 45 minutes, and after losing three engines, the skipper was forced to ditch. Incredibly no one was killed and only one crewman seriously wounded. The aircraft was like a colander; after all, they were armed with 37 mm and 20 mm cannons and all we had were machine guns. Anyway, after they left us, we took to our dinghies (three), but*

shortly after, two collapsed, holed by shrapnel, and eleven of us had to cram into one six-man dinghy. Fortunately, a Catalina found us during the night and homed some British warships on to us—the same ships who sank U504 and picked up the survivors of U461. (We had dropped one of our dinghies to the survivors of U461 after the attack when we saw them struggling in the water). As a matter of interest, the captain of the Catalina was a Scot by the name of John Cruikshank. A few weeks later, he was awarded the VC for a battle he had with a U-boat. He sank it, and, badly wounded, he got his aircraft back to base. He was whipped into hospital, and they picked 72 bits of shrapnel out of him! He is still alive, living in Aberdeen. I had correspondence with him recently—tough people, these Scots!

After the war I managed to locate Wolf Stiebler, the commandant of U461, and we became good friends. Rosemary and I visited him in Munich four times and he came out here in 1988 and spent Christmas with us. Sadly, he died a few years ago. I am still in touch with another four of them in Heidenheim. I also searched for the man who was given the credit for shooting us down: Willi Gutersmann. After the war, he was a solicitor in Frankfurt, but, unfortunately, he died before I could make contact. On my trips to Germany, I have made lots of friends. I remember at a reunion of old maritime flyers in Regensburg, sitting near a Dornier pilot drinking litre steins of beer, my mate turned to me and said, 'Peter, what a pity we didn't meet like this in 1939, then that stupid war would never have happened'—how true!

Hope you can follow my ramblings.
Give my regards to Lindy.
Cheers
Peter

Many articles have been written about Peter's crew of Australians serving in the 461 Squadron of the RAF.

Photo taken from the cockpit of the German fighter aircraft.
Peter and his crew are on the starboard wing with life rafts.
Port wing is underwater.

~

That darn trailer must have had nine lives. When driving off the vehicular ferry from Fraser Island at low tide, the drawbar of the bus dragged but appeared to be okay after a quick inspection. Our destination that day was Kingaroy, via some of Queensland's best farming and grazing country and typical rural towns with classic Queenslander-style elevated houses and big wide streets. While plodding along south of Goomeri after a leisurely lunch stop in Kilkivan, a police car with lights flashing pulled us over. I was nervous when walking behind the bus to talk with the policeman but couldn't think of anything I was doing wrong.

He said, 'Driver, do you notice anything missing?'

The trailer was gone, and I hadn't noticed it until then. My first panicked response was, 'Is anyone hurt?' Luckily, the answer was no.

The officer asked us to go back to the police station in Goomeri to sort out issues and do police paperwork.

Back in Goomeri, we found the trailer undamaged and parked neatly outside the police station. I thanked them for parking it there for me and they told me they hadn't moved it at all. It was exactly where it stopped when it came off. Apparently, as we drove through town, it broke away and skidded to a stop right outside the station. The police saw it happen because they were sitting out on the veranda having lunch, but when we didn't stop, they radioed to a patrol car down the highway and asked the officer to turn us back.

I discovered that some bolts had sheared off when the drawbar dragged earlier that day. The police recommended a mobile mechanic, and with the repair done quickly, I asked for an invoice, only to be told it would be sent by post. I questioned his trust towards a stranger and felt proud of the answer. 'I see the name Bishop on the side of the bus, and that's good enough for me.' After WWI, two of my grandfather's brothers moved to Queensland, and people in that area held their families in high regard.

Later that same tour when driving slowly through Surat, an overzealous local storekeeper ran out into the middle of the road to block our progress and demanded we stop in his town to see the new Cobb and Co Museum. Politely I explained we didn't have time, but he went off at me for depriving my passengers of the experience. His unique method of tourism promotion—or demotion—failed on that occasion, but when we came through with the next tour, I thought it best to bypass the main street to avoid another stand-off. My recollection of the incident amused my passengers as we drove the back-street detour and even more so when the CB radio barked into life with his barrage of abuse for not stopping.

After completing about twenty Cape York tours, we saw an opportunity for expansion into the Kimberley region of Western Australia, departing from Darwin and ending in Alice Springs. The first tour went well despite two issues with the bus: a snapped front-drive axle leaving us stranded in deep sand for twenty-four hours, and a blown tyre near Halls Creek. Normally, a blown tyre wouldn't be a big issue, but our bus had different front and rear wheel stud patterns, a legacy of its conversion to 4WD several years before, so we carried two spares. The spare for the front had already been used, so our only option was to swap a tyre from one rim to the other.

Shortly after pulling over to fix the problem, an empty bus bound for Halls Creek came along, and the driver offered to take everyone into town where they could wait more comfortably. Lindy went with them, and they drove off into the distance, disappearing into a heat mirage and leaving me alone in the middle of nowhere to battle with the tyres. A dozen or so black kites circled above like vultures, making shrill noises and crowding the airspace, and a lone crow making an unhelpful assessment of my situation soon joined them. I looked up and said, 'I know, mate.'

A truck approached, and my spirits lifted when it pulled up behind and old Merv got out to help me just like truckies did in the old days. He showed me a simple trick to break the tyre bead from the rim by driving onto it with the front wheel of his prime mover. With his help, we got the job finished in no time, so I invited him to join us for dinner in Halls Creek. He followed me into town, where I found Lindy working in the kitchen of the roadhouse preparing dinner for our group and helping with the evening rush. Merv received a well-deserved hero's welcome.

Before starting out across the Tanami Desert next morning, I bought two new tyres in Halls Creek and had them fitted to the steer axle to insure against any further tyre problems. But after a day on the Tanami and setting up camp on the Western Australia / Northern Territory border, I noticed one of the new tyres had a massive bulge. Fearing both new tyres could be troublesome, I began the backbreaking job, all over again, of changing tyres from rim to rim.

While I worked away, Margaret Whitely, a retired schoolteacher from our hometown of Shoalhaven Heads, prompted everyone to change their watches to Northern Territory time before going to bed. Next morning, we packed up camp in the dark and headed off on the long drive to Alice Springs, but after an hour or two, someone commented that the sun was a bit late rising. We had messed up the time-change calculation.

In the Alice next day, I claimed warrantee on the new tyres bought two days earlier at Halls Creek. The codes stamped on them indicated that they were at least twenty years old.

With two more new tyres fitted, we set off to deadhead the bus 2,350 kilometres to Cairns with Margaret Whitely along with us for the experience. It was a bit close quarters sleeping in the bus, especially after what we'd eaten for dinner that first night. Lindy rummaged through whatever we had with us and cooked dinner on a campfire using quite a lot of cabbage. Though we sat around the campfire watching the glorious outback sunset near Camooweal, that night was a very long, uncomfortable night for all of us.

Occasionally, the dry season's program finished in Alice Springs, so we programmed a Red Centre tour back from Alice Springs to Sydney to avoid bringing the bus all the way home empty. One leg of that tour was an easy 730 kilometres run from Ayres Rock to Coober Pedy. At lunchtime we pulled into a roadside rest area seventy kilometres north of Marla Bore, where I noticed a wheel-bearing problem with the trailer. I didn't have new bearings with me, so I left the group with the trailer to enjoy a leisurely lunch while I dashed into Marla to get a bearing set. Two hours later I returned, fitted the bearings and beckoned everyone back on board. To my surprise all I got was unified protest. They were playing a tense game of lawn bowls with the paddy melons that grew plentifully there and couldn't leave until they'd finished the game.

Gathering firewood along the Oodnadatta Track, South Australia.

After each long season of bashing the gear across tens of thousands of kilometres of corrugations and bulldust, twisting through tight gullies, scraping under low tree branches, pushing scores of loaded shopping trolleys out of supermarkets, dealing with hundreds of people and working hard physically in the heat and humidity of the tropics, we got a bit tired. Our relief to be deadheading for home at the end of the long season was like being on holiday. We drove the maximum permissible hours, finding it much easier and convenient to sleep in the bus at night rather than search out accommodation. The only issue was finding a quiet place to park in the darkness. Often, we were amused to see next morning where we had unknowingly parked.

Like in a quarry, a driveway into a cattle station, a vineyard and one night beside a cane field that was set on fire during the night. The flames scared the daylights out of us.

Sometimes the support crew travelled along behind us, and one night we stopped on the outskirts of a small inland Queensland town on rodeo night. Just after nodding off into a very deep sleep, Dave the Yowie, a crew member, banged on the side of the bus, desperate to move to another place right away.

'We can't stay here,' he said in a pleading tone. 'They're playing Hank Williams.'

He stormed off into the scrub with his swag. Apparently, kangaroos bounded around him all night and a train went right past him on the track he hadn't noticed.

One feature of that bus caused constant intrigue. When it was converted to 4WD, some of the modified machinery components encroached into the passenger compartment behind the driver, so a small section of the floor had to be raised. This meant that the person in the seat behind it had a step of about six inches higher than the rest of the floor on which to rest their feet. Human nature is hard to understand sometimes, because if someone sat there saying it was the best seat in the bus, it seemed everyone wanted to sit there. However, if the first person sitting there commented that it was a poor seat, nobody sat there.

Another side of human nature surfaced. It seemed that whenever an issue occurred with our older bus, passengers were unforgiving, even though older machines are much better suited to outback work. They are less complex, having no electronics to worry about and built much stronger. Importantly, the driver can tell when something is going wrong by vibrations and noises, which gives plenty of warning in time to arrange repairs before any failure. Even so, I knew we needed to update our bus to keep the confidence of our customers.

In the year 2000, we bit the bullet and ordered our first brand-new bus.

4

MAN That's Good!
The First New Bus

(2000 – 2006)

I read an article in the *Australian Bus and Coach Magazine* about four new 4WD buses being built for Sid Melksham, the owner of the Eurong Beach Resort on Fraser Island. Sid pioneered tours on the island and was well known in the industry as being very astute and having many years of hands-on experience with machinery. The new buses were forty feet long and on German MAN (Maschinenfabrik Augsburg Nurnberg) 4WD chassis. I figured if Sid thought those machines were worth buying, then I might have a look at them myself.

I flew to Brisbane, saw them in construction and placed my order for a similar machine. It was a huge move but one that we simply had to make, especially with so many bookings held for the year 2000. As always, working capital was scarce, so we advertised the old bus for sale, hoping it would sell before delivery of the new one. To our surprise, it sold quickly to a person intending to convert it into a motorhome. Hopefully the new bus would be delivered in time for an early start next season.

Serious problems exaggerated by the corrosive and abrasive environment of beach driving on Fraser Island riddled Sid's first vehicle. Salt water got into the complex electronics, causing extensive damage, and his first bus was a disaster. Modifications to avoid the same problems delayed the delivery of our bus for several months. In the meantime, we had no vehicle, and nothing was available for hire due to the busy Olympic year ahead for the bus industry. A local bus operator John King came to our rescue by selling us one of his Denning Landseer coaches. The Denning Landseer three-axle coach was well suited to outback touring, being very strongly built and sharing most of its major mechanical components with Kenworth trucks. Many operators, including me, believe they were the pinnacle of the Australian-built product, even to this day.

John had recently bought Nowra Coaches from the Gill family, with whom we were very close friends, and he amalgamated that with Pioneer Motor Services acquired from the Haigh/Kennedy family, also well known to us. I had long admired the vehicle we bought. Fleet number 49 was 'king of the road' when delivered to the Haighs' in time for the World Expo in Brisbane in 1988. Our plan was to start the season with 49 until our new MAN was built, then use it to do the job Coral Coaches were doing for us out of Cairns. It would be underutilised, but we figured it would be a good standby vehicle if we ever needed one in a hurry, and it could be put on charter to the Sydney Olympic Committee to earn good money later in the year.

To start the new season in the year 2000, we deadheaded the Landseer to Alice Springs using this valuable time to become acquainted with the six-speed Spicer 'crash' gearbox with reversed shift pattern and 'around-the-corner' overdrive. Once familiar, I found it easier to shift gears without using the clutch, just like in my old truckie days.

Number 49.

On the 2,700 kilometre trip, like all the deadheading trips we ever did, Lindy sat up behind me and chatted all day about work, family, friends and so on. We both enjoyed these times in each other's company. At night we stopped at roadhouses for a shower and meal, then slept under the coach in the luggage bins.

In Alice Springs our base was the Gapview Hotel and campground, just inside the Heavitree Gap at the southern entrance to town. Here, we parked securely off the street, pitched our tent, used one of the coach bay kitchens or went to the pub for meals. On rare occasions, if it was cold or wet, we treated ourselves to a hotel room and sometimes had the very same suite where Prince Charles and Lady Diana stayed when visiting Alice Springs in 1983. Greyhound tours also used Gapview as their base, and they let us use their wash bay, toilet dump point and sump oil tanks.

When the new MAN finally left the Brisbane factory, Billy Gill deadheaded it 3,600 kilometres to Kununurra in Western Australia to rendezvous with us halfway through an eighteen-day Kimberley tour. Passengers were as excited as us when boarding the brand-new machine to continue their tour down the Gibb River Road. Billy then drove 49 directly to Cairns, three thousand kilometres away, and parked it ready for use later that year.

The new machine handled the rough roads brilliantly, being much smoother, quieter and way more fuel efficient than 49. Its off-road capacity was impressive with constant 4WD, front and rear diff locks, planetary hub drives, two-speed transfer case and the longest leaf springs on any machine I ever saw. I loved driving it, and our passengers commented on how comfortable it was.

The new bus at the Bungle Bungles, Western Australia.

I learned in that first week, though, that putting a brand-new vehicle straight into service without having a 'shake-down' period or chance to find and fix any manufacturing faults beforehand was not a good idea. All major components performed perfectly, but it had numerous minor issues. First, a faulty luggage door latch that I noticed when a trail of luggage items fell out the back. We backtracked several kilometres, picking up items all along the way and, luckily, nobody lost anything. A couple of days later, when driving between Fitzroy Crossing and Halls Creek, an enormous explosion under the floor near Lindy's seat frightened her so much that she dived back into the aisle. Just under the floor was a huge, four-cylinder, belt-driven air-conditioning compressor—the biggest unit we could buy in Australia when speccing-up the new bus. A 200-amp, 24-volt alternator to generate power for the air-conditioning system was mounted beside it, and the whole assembly sat on rubber blocks for noise and vibration suppression. The problem was that no earth strap had been fitted, so the wire-braided refrigerant hoses were earthing the whole system. Constant arcing inside the pressurised hoses inevitably caused one to fail, and off it blew.

In the heat of the afternoon and with the A/C not working, we reached Halls Creek, holding very little hope of finding anyone to fix it. I was desperate because our tight schedule compelled an early start next morning for the two-day crossing of the Tanami Desert to Alice Springs. Without air conditioning the drive was impossible, not just for temperature comfort, but to maintain enough positive cabin pressure to keep dust out. I wasn't going to do it without the A/C, so I contemplated doing a 1,350 kilometres round trip overnight back to Broome for repairs to keep on schedule. By chance I noticed a hand-painted sign in the distance advertising refrigerator repairs, and with no real hope that they could do automotive repairs, I asked the question anyway. You wouldn't believe our luck, but they did. The failed hose was just long enough to cut off the burned section and re-use what remained. Incredibly the fittings weren't crimped but threaded, and so could be re-used. The repaired system was evacuated and re-gassed right there on the side of the road in Halls Creek.

The new bus took a couple of years to fully settle down, but every time an issue arose, our passengers were understanding and even sympathetic. They said the problems weren't foreseeable and shouldn't have happened with a new machine. It had body struts crack, windows that shook loose, exhaust issues and some major service points had been panelled over by the body builders without any real thought given.

~

95

Crossing the Tanami Desert always caused me anxiety, not helped when confronted by several large warning signs at the start of the Tanami Road. One warned of no fuel or services, another indicated where road closures might be and a third was a milepost displaying the distance to Alice Springs—1,060 kilometres. The passengers relished a quick stop here to photograph the bus parked alongside the signs and facing the long red gravel road ahead.

I loved my job and enjoyed the feeling of excitement building in the bus, but I worried about the risks we were about to undertake. Thorough preparation was the best way to mitigate these risks, and when easing the bus out onto the rough road and shifting up through the gears again, I ran through the checklist—yes, fuel tanks and jerry cans were full; water tanks and every water container in the bus were full; Bruce and Jackie Farrands at Rabbit Flat knew we were coming; road and weather conditions were checked and favourable; passengers were fit, well and had whatever medications needed with them; satellite phone was fully charged and several passengers trained to use it and so on.

For the first forty kilometres, the Tanami Road winds through typical Kimberley cattle country of undulating grasslands crossed by many gullies that require some caution, especially where traversing the road with steep dips and tyre shredding, cricket-ball-sized rocks at the bottom. Then it tracks out across a black-soil plain adjacent to the Ruby Plains station, one of the string of properties once owned by Sir Sidney Kidman, the famous 'cattle king' and the last one in Western Australia still operated by S Kidman and Co. Eventually the landscape becomes wide and flat and speed can be increased enough to find the 'sweet spot' where the machine rides happiest over the corrugations—sixty to eighty kilometres per hour.

After four hours driving and at the 150 kilometres mark, we reached the Wolfe Creek Meteorite Crater, always a welcome and fascinating place to take a break. Most people were surprised to see it, because from a distance it looks just like a low ridge. But a short, steep walk up onto the rim gives a full view of its immensity. A meteor weighing seventeen thousand tons slammed into earth here 120,000 years ago, leaving a crater nine hundred metres wide and sixty metres deep and the second biggest on Earth. Despite it being so big, people with European ancestry didn't recognise it as a crater until it was seen from the air in the 1940s. For the Aborigines it held spiritual significance as the place where the rainbow serpent came out of the earth and slithered away, forming Sturt Creek.

The road south of the crater runs through endless kilometres of flat country covered with saltbush or spinifex and with innumerable large termite mounds. Occasionally it runs between tall sandhills, and often we saw feral camels and donkeys. But just as drivers get comfortable out there, they can hit axle-breaking ruts hidden under stretches of deep bulldust, and in other places, if they encounter soft sandy sections at high speed, vehicles can decelerate so quickly that the force of it throws passengers forward in their seats.

Many car wrecks, mostly old Holdens and Falcons, lie off to the side, right where they died, and millions of empty beer cans are strewn beside the road in such numbers that we knew when the border was getting close because the colour of the cans changed from the black and red of Western Australia's Swan Lager to the green VB cans preferred in the Territory.

In that isolation, self-sufficiency for all foreseeable circumstances is essential. Initially we carried an HF radio for emergency contact with the outside world, but in later years, satellite phones took over this role. The bus had a UHF radio mounted in it, enabling communication with drivers of the huge, slow-moving 140-ton road-train leviathans that stirred up so much dust that it could blind drivers behind for several kilometres back. Overtaking was impossible in these conditions, but road-train drivers were mostly good blokes and let us past if we radioed to let them know we were behind them in the dust.

We relied on the support of Bruce and Jackie Farrands, the operators of Australia's most remote roadhouse at Rabbit Flat just south of the Western Australia/Northern Territory border. Bruce lived and worked out there long before establishing the roadhouse in 1969, and the nearby Mt Farrands was named after him. Jackie first met Bruce when touring Australia as a French tourist and visited Rabbit Flat with legendary outback coach operators Bill and Doreen Hand of Sundowner Coach Tours.

The actual Rabbit Flat is a dry lakebed ten kilometres from the roadhouse where, in the wetter climates of the Ice Ages, deep lake water sustained a thriving marine eco system.

The roadhouse was like nothing we'd ever seen before. Built as a fortress, it enabled Bruce and Jackie to lock themselves securely inside if they ever felt threatened by thirsty locals from dry communities or dubious road users. All customer service was through a small, barred servery window, like that of a jail cell, and every conversation we ever had with Jackie was either through the bars or by phone. They had twin sons, both of whom joined the army, where one of them became a commando—no doubt their toughness was a result of a spartan upbringing.

On one of our very early Tanami crossings, we stopped at Rabbit Flat to see an interesting exchange between Bruce and a customer at the fuel bowser. A city bloke was mouthing-off about the high price of the fuel, so Bruce didn't say a word but just locked the bowser and strolled back inside, refusing to sell him any. Straight after the incident, I pulled the coach up to the bowser and asked for it to be filled right up. It was important to cement strong relationships and support the service providers in remote areas because we relied on them as much as they relied on us. Bruce thanked me, and from that time on we got on especially well.

Before ever heading into the Tanami with a tour group, I routinely phoned Rabbit Flat for the latest road and weather reports and to ask if we could bring anything out from town for them as we came. Every Christmas Bruce and Jackie sent us a card with a thank you note enclosed.

Our main campsite on the Tanami was several kilometres from the Rabbit Flat Roadhouse at the gateway to Mongrel Downs Station. The big level area surrounded by mulga gave shelter from prevailing winter desert winds, and we enjoyed the clear, dark desert skies more here than anywhere else because we could see the flat horizon in all directions.

If we were making slower progress and couldn't reach Rabbit Flat in daylight, we used a campsite we called Number 44 Tanami Road, hidden well off the road in the scrub. The turn-off into the site was marked by a forty-four-gallon drum filled with sand out on the side of the lonely road. Another campsite we used, if coming from the other direction, was 'Grader Camp' just south of the Granites mines.

In later years as mobile phones and phone towers became more common, it always amused us to hear mobile phones dinging right out in the middle of nowhere as we went past the Granites gold mines. Passengers lunged for their phones, but the signal only lasted for ten minutes.

Up near the tip of Cape York, we had a strong bond with Dan

and Patsy Lennox, who we first met when they managed the Red Island Point Campground at Seisia. On one of our many visits, Dan looked a bit preoccupied and eventually told me his tenure over the campground had been cancelled. He asked if I had time to go with him for a quick drive to look at a possible alternate site he was hoping to develop. The site he showed me was quite magnificent, being right on the beach overlooking the Torres Strait. All he needed was a commitment of support from several commercial operators so his backers would confidently finance the project. In return for our loyalty, we could select the best campsite location, and it would be ours whenever we stayed. It was a good deal, so we shook hands.

The next season we arrived with the first bus group and couldn't believe what he'd achieved. In conjunction with the Islander community of New Mapoon, he'd built a brick amenity block and kiosk, and a thatched-roofed shelter large enough to seat forty people stood on our site. Commercial operators who'd shown loyalty to Dan and Patsy had streets in the new campground named after them—Duncan's Drive, Billy Tea Boulevard and Bishop's Terrace. The new campground was appropriately named Loyalty Beach, a name also significant to the Islanders as they'd originated from the Loyalty Islands near New Guinea, immigrating after WWII.

Later in the year 2000, like most others in Australia, Olympic excitement overwhelmed us. We'd committed both our coaches to the Sydney Olympics Organising Committee, and they sent our nominated drivers to instructional seminars—all except me. About a week before the opening ceremony, a person from the organising committee phoned and offered me the plumb job of railway replacement between Bomaderry and Dapto with 49, so, together with a mate Denis Thorpe, we operated that service for the duration. My shift started at two in the morning with all stations to Dapto, then all stations back to Bomaderry, arriving back around eight in the morning, then I stood by at home just in case there were any issues with the train system. Denis then took over at two in the afternoon to do the same run but stand by for several hours at Dapto. We left the new 4WD MAN bus pooled in Sydney, and it regularly ran to Canberra.

For me, it was a real eye opener, because I'd never realised how the other half lived. One morning at 2:00 am, I parked at the station and a fellow looking a little 'under the influence' approached me. He asked if I would open the luggage bins so he could put some items underneath. A laden truck then pulled up alongside and several of his mates quickly filled the entire bin space with furniture, suitcases and cartons of various items. I was late departing because of this but eventually got going. Then, as I tried to make up time to get back on schedule, he came up front and asked if I could stop the bus so he could relieve himself outside. I kept the toilet on board locked to avoid misuse, so I did what he asked. On arrival at Oak Flats Station, it took both of us about fifteen minutes to unload all his stuff out onto the footpath. I often wonder what he did with all those items after I left, or even if it was his stuff.

Later that night as I waited at Dapto Station, several very young girls left the nearby Dapto Leagues Club and climbed onto the coach. As we departed, one of them said she was cold and asked for the heaters to be turned up. I replied that I wasn't surprised she was cold wearing what she was—with a great deal of skin showing. Before starting the Olympic work, the organising committee explicitly told us not to deviate from the set route or stop anywhere other than the railway stations, not under any circumstances, but on this occasion I did. On arrival in Kiama, I simply couldn't see them walk safely for several kilometres along dark streets at that time of the morning, so I let them off close to their homes. I bet their fathers didn't know what they were up to.

Working for the Sydney Olympics Organising Committee was a very rewarding time financially, but more importantly, it gave us the opportunity to make some very useful contacts in the bus industry. The media was actively chasing stories, and our new 4x4 coach caught the attention of a journalist from the *Australasian Bus and Coach Magazine* when he spotted it on the Canberra to Sydney service. A later issue featured our new machine on the front cover. The caption read 'BRUCE BISHOP'S GO ANYWHERE COACH' with a photo of the new four-wheel-drive bus fording the Wenlock River on Cape York. I felt a little overwhelmed by all the attention.

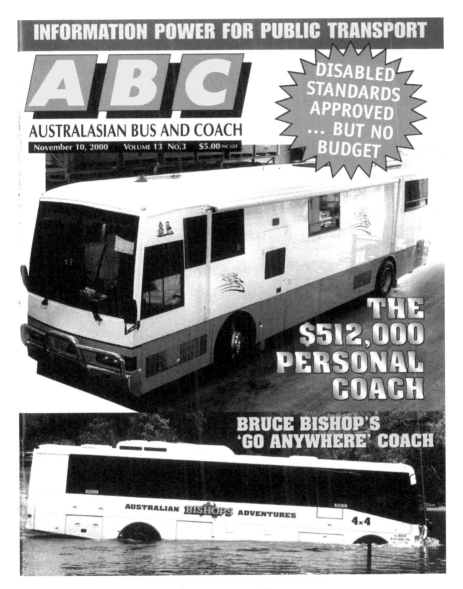

The Magazine Cover

With 49 in our operation, we started running tours to numerous, less adventurous places and scheduled trips all year round using motel accommodation more often. Each year started with two trips to Tamworth for the Country Music Festival. An old school mate, Peter Roberts, was the council officer in charge of the festival, and he helped us get the use of a river front camp site just two hundred metres from the city Visitors' Information Centre. We established the camp much more substantially for the two-week period, erecting cabin tents up off the ground on timber bases and adding carpets and electric lights inside.

The last trip each year was to the popular Carols in the Caves performance at the Jenolan Caves, where we always filled both coaches and booked out most of the motel rooms in Oberon. On the drive home after this show, I always had the same feeling I remember from the last day of school before the Christmas holidays.

During this time, we added tours to Gippsland, Tasmania, Great Ocean Road, the Grampians, Corner Country, Innamincka and Birdsville, the Eyre Peninsula and Flinders Ranges, Goldfields and Pilbara in Western Australia, Gulf Savannah, Carnarvon Gorge and Bunya Mountains, Longreach and outback Queensland, Lightning Ridge and the Warrumbungles, plus many extended tours and day charters, mostly for Probus Clubs.

Each new tour required a lot of planning and research on things like where to stay, what highlights to include, where to stop for morning teas and lunches, and all the interesting things to learn so I could give informative commentaries. Sometimes we flew to the nearest big city and hired a 4WD or, better still, booked a tour with a local operator.

After a while we realised that the same tours were often charged at different prices depending on the perceived capacity of customers to pay. For example, a tour booked from a classy resort could be quite expensive, but the same tour booked from a backpacker's hostel would be much cheaper. With this in mind, we booked a day tour along the Great Ocean Road at the YHA hostel in Melbourne, expecting to be picked up in a luxury coach along with all the folk staying with us at the hotel. Big mistake. We were jammed into a little Coaster bus with fifteen teenagers and scared stiff by the young driver's lack of attention as he fooled around trying to impress the girls on board. After about half an hour of this dangerous behaviour, he passed around a microphone and asked everyone to say their name, where they came from and what they did. When my turn came, I mentioned I was an Australian and also a transport inspector for the Victorian Transport Department. You wouldn't believe how he changed.

~

For twenty-five years, the Probus Club of Epping travelled with us to every corner of Australia, and a great, very capable bloke named Wal did all their arrangements. First it was Wal Maizey, then Wal Cooper, followed by Wal Gallagher, and we admired all the Wals immensely. We became very fond of all those travelling with us from Epping, especially Wal.

Wal Maizey led a group to meet us in Cairns, and from there we showed them the Daintree, Cape Tribulation, Cooktown, Lakefield NP and the Atherton Tablelands. After a big day in the rough and tumble of the Lower Cape, we stayed in the very basic Lakeland Downs Motel, shared that night with a rowdy crew of road workers. Lindy and I were so busy preparing a BBQ dinner that we hadn't been to our room before finishing work at ten in the evening.

When finally opening the door into our room, Lindy

exclaimed, 'There's someone in the bed.'

A voice came back out of the darkness, 'Yes, but there's room for one more, love.'

Another time when we toured Far West New South Wales with them, we were stranded for nearly a day at the historic Daydream Silver Mine near Broken Hill. The six kilometre access track to the mine site crossed a wide, dry creek bed and wound through a very picturesque dusty red landscape leading to the mine, where Lindy served morning tea beside the bus. To the north we noticed an unusual crimson, blue-grey, wave-like cloud formation rolling in towards us, an intriguing sight because it spanned from ground level to high altitude. It reminded me of the time I drove the Mack through a dust storm, so I urged everybody back onto the bus and shut the door. Within seconds a violent windstorm rocked the bus and peppered it with leaves, branches, sand and dust before day turned into night, and the heavens opened. Rain pelted down like a waterfall and thunder clapped all around. We huddled in the bus for half an hour, hoping the window glass could cope with the barrage, then, as quickly as it hit us, it was gone. We stepped off the bus into sunshine, but everywhere we looked, the gullies ran full of water between the low hills.

The mine caretaker guide, Gary, drove me back along the access road to where the wide creek crossing was now a raging torrent of muddy floodwaters carrying debris and logs, making any attempts to cross impossible. Stranded, we settled into the café and discussed the possibility of spending the night—unless we could charter a helicopter. After several hours we inspected the crossing again and saw the levels dropping, so optimism grew about attempting a later crossing. Gary, anxious and fidgety, made some outrageous suggestions, like hitching the bus behind his backhoe loader tractor and dragging us through the creek.

A good idea with an experienced, cool-headed tractor driver but not with a 'loose cannon' driving—he would surely pull the front off the bus, leaving us in an even bigger predicament. He became insistent, so I compromised to avoid a clash of wills. Just before sundown he drove over the crossing ahead of the bus with the tractor bucket clearing any obstructions, then waited on the opposite bank in case we needed a tow. I asked everyone to stay seated and try to remain calm. With low gear and front and rear diff locks engaged, I steered the bus into the water—now running much slower but still a metre deep. The hardest part was climbing out on the other side because Gary got his tractor in our way, causing us to lose momentum. We just managed to crawl out with all four wheels spinning.

~

I remember the first time my accountant told me that we had a tax problem. Usually, he looked at me over the top of his glasses, fiddling with his pen and talking awkwardly about our financial situation.

On his advice we purchased an industrial block in Bomaderry with a large bus shed and workshop, and a nice house on five acres at Meroo Meadow, just a short drive from the new depot. Even though we now lived in a nice house, just like Crocodile Dundee, we couldn't break our outdoor living habits when at home. Most meals we enjoyed al fresco on the back porch and even cooked toast for breakfast on the BBQ, just like on tour. Our boys all moved to Sydney for work and often brought a girlfriend home for the weekend. Joe turned up one weekend with a girl related to the great Steve Rogers (NRL star player). In conversation she said how she hated football because it had dominated her family life for as long as she could recall and was only with Joe because he was retired. My response was one of total surprise and disbelief, and I made the comment, without thinking, that footballers never retire; they just get too old to play anymore.

At breakfast next morning, out on the back porch, I asked her how she liked her toast.

'How do you mean?' she asked.

I replied, 'Well, you can have it cold and chewy or hot and crispy.'

'You seem to know an awful lot about toast,' she said.

So I got a pen and paper and did a calculation. I routinely cooked more than half a ton of toast each year.

~

Eventually, we bought a second support truck and equipped it with Bush Lodge equipment the same as the original one and recruited another crew for the coming season. It was easy getting a crew together because people saw the job as a good opportunity to travel and to experience adventurous outback itineraries. Usually, applicants had no concept of how gruelling the season was, especially being constantly on the move in the heat and humidity of the tropics. If they ever signed up for a second season, it became just a job. Very few ever lasted to the third year, and it was surprising how many people were unable to cope when put under pressure. Just like on the rugby field, the cream really does rise to the top when people are placed in this situation. My old mate Bruno took his annual leave from TAFE each year, where he held a management position, and he worked to the point where he could barely stand up, then he turned up again, day after day, to do the same. Another who lasted well was Denis Thorpe. He worked with us for quite a few seasons.

Often as crews tired through the season, we recruited additional help for them by pinning a note in backpacker hostels in either Cairns or Alice Springs that advertised a unique opportunity to travel for free and earn some cash. This was very successful because we gained the extra help and gave our passengers a chance to relate very happily with these young folk. Some passengers even invited some of them back to private homes in the weeks and months after a tour.

For the winter season in 2001, we were very fortunate to have a recently retired bus operator, John Craig, working with us and driving 49. Before retirement, John operated John Craig's Buffalo Tours out of Swansea, and bus operators regarded him highly. We first met him several years before when he was selling a 4WD bus, and in the years that followed, we learned a great deal from him, particularly when contemplating tours to places with which we were not well acquainted. He told us of all the highlights, where best to camp or stay and introduced us to many of the important contacts. When all this was done, he reviewed it all, and when he was happy, we were confident to proceed.

John was also very lively company, and still displayed the quick-witted cheekiness of the champion halfback he once was. In his youth he played and coached rugby league at a high level, playing two hundred first-grade games for Lakes United and representing Newcastle against the New Zealand national side. He was not a big man, but he did everything energetically and at full speed, and even after a big day behind the wheel, he could still rally himself to recite a bush poem or sing a song.

That season of 2001 was one of the smoothest running we'd ever had, with John welcoming our passengers in Cairns, then bringing them up the Cape as far as Weipa in 49. There, we swapped groups to keep the 4X4 coach in the more challenging conditions and allow double passenger numbers each season.

By September, the last Cape York tour group of the season was northbound out of Weipa on the 4WD coach, and around noon on the thirteenth of September 2001, we arrived at the Jardine River Ferry. We'd been out of contact with the outside world for two days, and it was here that we first heard of the 9/11 attacks on the USA two days before.

I went numb all over when contemplating what this could mean for the world and our business, plus the eighty people we had in our care at that time on the two coaches. How could we get everyone home if flights were grounded? And could we survive any dramatic travel downturn, especially now that we were committed to another new coach without having sold 49?

I tuned the HF radio to Radio Australia and channelled it through the bus speaker system so we could all hear about the alarming events occurring in the outside world.

A quiet and very subdued group camped that night in Bishops Terrace at Loyalty Beach.

Later in the evening, when most of our group had gone to bed, Lindy and I took a walk along the beach. The night was totally still and the waters of the Torres Strait so calm that they reflected the galactic lighting as if in a mirror. The moon hung low in the sky and cast a beam of light across the ocean surface brighter than we'd ever seen before, and Venus was so bright it also reflected over the surface. Emotionally exhausted, we stood there on the beach, gazing up at this celestial light show, a splendorous sight we'd never seen before and have never seen since. We saw it as a reminder that we were in the care of a much greater power, and the stunning sight was His assurance we would be okay.

5

Man Verses MAN.
The Second New Bus

(2002 – 2004)

Maybe a thousand times, passengers asked me what the letters MAN on the front of the bus stood for? The proper answer is 'Maschinenfabrik Augsburg-Nurnberg' but after a short time operating our second new MAN bus, I changed the answer to 'Mechanics Always Needed' or 'Many Adjustments Necessary'.

Early in 2002, bookings were going nuts, and we were not so much running the business as responding to the demand. The big Denning Landseer vehicle we called 49 was working much harder in our operation than we'd ever intended, and it was costing a fortune on fuel. It had a big thirsty V692 GM 2-stroke Silver 350 diesel and a 900-litre fuel tank. By this time, it had clocked up 1,290,000 kilometres since it was built in 1988, so we contemplated its replacement.

When we acquired 49, the intention was to schedule it on the back-to-back portion of the Kimberley and Cape York tours, then have it on standby just in case we ever had a major breakdown or accident with the MAN 4WD. However, it proved too costly to have a vehicle with such substantial overheads just sitting around.

Many passengers who enjoyed their trips to Cape York or the Kimberley wanted to go somewhere else with us and, within a very short time, we had a healthy mailing list compiled of several thousand previous travellers. We rapidly introduced back-to-back overlapping itineraries to Cape York, the Kimberley, Gulf Savannah, Corner Country and Tasmania. Using this system allowed us to participate in every tour personally and opened the opportunity for many more tours each season.

Our accountant kept telling us to upgrade the vehicles, so in early September 2001, we ordered our second new bus, another MAN, but this time with a Denning body. It broke my heart to see 49 leave us, but the new replacement was simply gorgeous. I took delivery in Brisbane in early 2002 and headed for home via the New England Highway. As I started out, the joy of owning a machine like this was overwhelming. Powerful, quiet and smooth, it had that intoxicating new-vehicle smell—but also an occasional thump under the back whenever it hit a bump, and that became a little annoying after a while. *Oh well, I'll fix it when I get home.*

By the end of the delivery trip, I had quite a list of things to check and fix and was thankful not to have forty passengers on board like we had with the previous new coach. This time, all the issues were MAN-related, the body being completely trouble free. Not a problem; I planned to work through the list in the weeks ahead and be on top of things before its first tour to Birdsville via Camerons Corner.

The first day having passengers aboard started routinely with a 'milk run' up the coast, picking up passengers along the way, then through the city via Sutherland, Hurstville and Strathfield. Excitement levels were greater than usual on this day due to the new bus, and the normally busy process was a little more hectic and confused. At Strathfield, Lindy gave me the all-clear signal to get underway after accounting for everybody on the manifest. About half an hour later, she answered a desperate phone call from one of the passengers still back at Strathfield. Apparently, he'd checked in with Lindy, then among all the excitement at the bus stop, he'd gone back to use the station amenities and not told anyone. That was the only time we ever left a passenger behind.

The long steep climb up the Blue Mountains had the new, fully-laden machine working hard for the first time, and I monitored the gauges keenly to see how it was coping. We quickly left Sydney's sprawling suburbs behind, replaced by sandstone mountains covered in eucalyptus bush with the distinctive blue hue in the heat of the day. I smelled paint burning off the new engine, as expected as temperatures rose, then the entire dashboard went berserk, flickering lights and gauge needles waving madly before the whole dash went dead. A quick check of the fuse panel showed all circuit breakers untripped. We limped blind into Bathurst, where Lindy served a picnic lunch while I found an auto electrician for help. After an hour or so tracing wiring looms, he found a loose plug. Just teething problems, I was sure, and the tour continued.

Next day out in the wide-open spaces west of Cobar, I wondered why the rev counter indicated steadily increasing engine revs while the speedo showed a steady 100 kph. Sitting high in the driver's seat of a heavy vehicle doesn't give the same sense of speed as in a car when sitting closer to the ground, and despite what the speedo indicated, I wondered if we were travelling a little quicker. When we pulled into Wilcannia substantially ahead of schedule, it confirmed my suspicion. A speed sensor malfunctioned, so we must've been doing 130 kph.

The new bus was like this its whole life, just one problem after another, but our passengers loved it. Fuel savings over the old 49 coach, however, almost paid the lease payments—one consolation.

New bus number two at The Devil's Marbles, Northern Territory.

Some months later on the eve of a Kimberley tour departing from Alice Springs, I broke out in a nasty rash from top to toe that a doctor diagnosed as stress related. I was sick with worry about the risks involved in taking a large group of mature-aged passengers out into the Tanami Desert with this fault-riddled machine. All I could do was get a copy of the Yellow Pages and compile a long list of all the options for emergency help and put a local bus operator on standby, just in case. Trouble struck on the way back to Alice Springs when the air compressor failed. Without compressed air, the brake system, clutch boost, gear box range change and door with retractable step were non-functional. We rigged an 'umbilical-cord' air hose from the support truck to transfer compressed air and limped the dud machine out of the desert for repairs.

Owning this bus became like a scene from Homer's Odyssey for me. I felt like Ulysses when lashed to the mast of the ship so he could resist the bewitching song of the Sirens. This bus had so much appeal, but it was luring and conspiring to destroy me.

When it was twelve months old, I reached the end of my tether and demanded a crisis meeting with the MAN bus division 'suits'. They arranged a meeting at our nearest MAN dealership in Nowra, and without their knowledge, my old Rotary mate and solicitor, Phil Broad, waited inconspicuously out the back in spare parts. When all were seated around the table, Phil burst in, dropped a printed copy of our demands in front of each of them and, with the benefit of surprise, attacked them with a masterful display of how we were going to castrate them if that bastard of a machine wasn't fixed—or that's how it seemed to me with all the big words he used. We laughed for years after that and likened it to a perfect rolling maul in rugby.

To be fair, that bus did a huge job for us over several years, but we never gave it a proper name because none of us ever felt any attachment to it. At one stage we contemplated naming our two buses, one after Lindy's mum, Nora, and the other after my mum, Norma, but whose name would we give to the bad one? I never pushed the idea further.

The two buses on The Gibb River Road, Western Australia.

Eventually the MAN people did the right thing and helped us get out of that machine. We replaced it with a little, near-new Mercedes/Denning we named Rebecca and used it just for local touring.

The problem bus was subsequently bought and sold many times and caused trouble wherever it went. It turned up for a while in Oberon, where we often saw it and, not that I cared, the last I heard, it was carrying schoolchildren on the South Coast, but never venturing more than a handful of kilometres from its depot.

~

During this time of being frantically busy, we assembled a great

116

group of people around us. In the office, Christine Corletto answered endless phone calls, responded to mail enquiries, did the banking, fed the dog (and retrieved her from the pound) and constantly worked on mailouts. Each mailout was so big it filled the ute and needed coordination with Sue and Michael at the post office to have enough space and people ready to process the load. Nobody could match Christine's speed when putting brochures into envelopes.

Out on the road, we had two wonderful bus crews sharing the workload with us—John and Yvonne Craig, and Ian and Shirley Salway. I'd known Ian since boyhood, when we travelled to school together in Porky Wilson's bus. For several years we also had Rod driving and Colleen (who we called Sam), as his hostess. Rod first started as support crew, then switched to the buses, making a big contribution with his mechanical skills.

We met and travelled with thousands of people and obviously couldn't remember all their names if we hadn't seen them for a while. For each tour Christine compiled a passenger list that noted any previous travellers and what tours they'd done with us. To help jog my memory, Lindy quizzed and tested me beforehand so I could at least greet them by their first names. After a while a pattern emerged that I mostly remembered either the very good or the very bad passengers quite well.

Some were just so special that I could never forget them. Gretchen was one, a very well-presented lady we first met on a tour chartered by the Royal Automobile Club of Sydney. In conversation one night, she remarked that if her first husband were still alive today, he would be 125 years old. I asked how many former husbands she'd had, and I must have looked surprised when she told me she'd had four husbands, because after dinner she took me quietly aside and said, 'But, Bruce, they all died of natural causes.'

Ken Godfrey was also on that trip from the RAC, and he joined us often after that. A very 'polished' man, he obviously lived life to the fullest. Ken introduced us to the music of Floyd Cramer, and twenty years later when visiting the historic Studio B at RCA Records in Nashville, I sat at the keyboard of Floyd's historic Steinway grand piano and said a quiet thank you to Ken. He was a Scots College old boy and apparently enjoyed meeting up each year for a reunion. When in his nineties on his last tour with us, he expressed his disappointment when only five of the lads bothered to turn up for the last reunion. I didn't pursue that conversation further.

Another character was Eric, who, after separating from his wife, cooked himself two lamb chops for dinner, six nights a week for seven years straight. His reason was simply that he liked lamb chops. Lindy often served lamb chops, and he always keenly sought an extra serve.

Keith and Anne Moses were also very special. Keith's mum, Edith, aged eighty-six years, was the oldest person we ever took to Cape York, then many years later, they booked four tours in succession—the Pilbara, Kimberley, Gulf and Cape York. This concerned me because outback touring is not for everyone, and we hoped they'd be happy in the rough and tumble routine for so long. I was, however, mostly concerned that they'd tire of my jokes during the evening announcements. We loved their company, but it was me who tired of Keith's jokes. When they left us in Cairns after the four tours, it seemed a little flat without them, but they travelled many more times and even came overseas with us years later.

We often chuckle when recalling Keith's bicycle accident in Belgium when he lost control and crashed through a rural fence in the countryside. Lying, apparently quite badly hurt, in the long, wet grass, he screamed at us not to move him because he was tingling and convulsing all over.

I said, 'Keith, you're lying on an electric fence wire.'

Luckily, his injuries were just to his ego, and we later laughed over a few cold Belgian Jupiler beers.

~

We mostly programmed our busy lives two years ahead. Alarmingly, hefty lease payments for machines depreciating almost as fast as we could pay for them gobbled up much of the financial rewards. We contemplated investing more in property, so started looking around for a new base where a busload of passengers could be accommodated and interesting day tours run each day so we could be home each night. We considered a large old guest house in Talbingo and several 'green fields' opportunities around Oberon but eventually found the perfect property at Little Forest, high up on the range behind Milton. The awesome location had spectacular coastal views, a pocket of rainforest with a spring-fed creek flowing through and a wall of sandstone cliffs towering behind.

The former H Ranch horse-riding school had very substantial buildings, but business suffered when horses were excluded from the National Park that adjoined the rear boundary. Also their once-popular woolshed dances held in the large central building lost popularity when random driver breath testing was introduced. We bought it quite cheaply using the money paid to us by MAN when they bought back the problem bus.

Our youngest son, Andy, a builder, spent a year or so bringing the newly named Little Forest Lodge back to life. He refurbished thirteen ensuite rooms along with large fireside lounging areas and a bar and dining room, and he built rainforest walks and viewing platforms.

119

Business continued as normal while Andy worked on the big project. One Saturday morning, we pulled up for morning tea in Mittagong with a group bound for Yerranderie, and I bought a copy of the Sydney Morning Herald. I read with interest about the refurbishment of the Sydney Hilton Hotel and a sale beforehand of all the contents. We acted quickly, booking a night there for later that week to see first hand what was being sold.

The housekeeping staff gave the best advice, 'Don't touch anything on the tenth floor because those rooms are used for Japanese groups who all smoke. Go to the sixteenth floor. The rooms were all updated recently with brand-new beds and furniture.'

We bought the whole sixteenth floor for four hundred dollars per room. Everything removable was ours—beds, blankets, TVs, clock radios, paintings, linen, curtains, chairs, lounges, electric kettles, marble bathroom-bench tops, brass bathroom fittings, floor rugs and so on, and all of it top quality and almost new. Getting all this out and down the elevators to the underground loading docks and onto trucks was a major task, especially in competition with all the other buyers. For each room purchased, the selling agents allocated us just fifteen minutes time at the loading docks two levels below Pitt Street. Like any bus operator would, I scheduled the trucks, drivers and helpers to a timetable that required a phone call if not met. Whenever a loaded truck left the dock, another waiting outside in Pitt Street moved in just like musical chairs. The supervisors at the Hilton were so impressed, they even whispered where spare items might be found on various other floors.

At our depot in Bomaderry, a team of 'gorillas' unloaded the trucks quickly while the drivers took their rest breaks, then when waiting for the next truckload to arrive, they sorted and packed items neatly away.

We lavishly furnished the thirteen guest rooms, lounge room and dining room at Little Forest Lodge with Hilton items, and from then on, called it The Milton Hilton. Some months later, we held a big sale to clear out all the surplus items from the depot so we could fit the buses back in. It yielded more than we paid for the whole lot.

Little Forest Lodge worked quite well, allowing us to give full-time employment to several key crew members, and it was good being at home a bit more. During the week we hosted our bus groups and at weekends often had wedding-group bookings. Of all the tasks we ever tackled, weddings were the hardest. I often commented that I would prefer to get out of bed early on a cold, wet Sunday morning after a big night out to milk cows rather than host weddings.

One time, fire damaged another local wedding venue, so to help them through, we took over one of their wedding bookings on the normal terms of payment one week prior to the event. We suspected trouble and that's what we got. First, the family made no payments on time, but eventually, when they understood the event was in jeopardy, several relatives clumped together to make multiple visa payments to reinstate the booking. Then, the father of the groom took me aside the day before to tell of the hostility between the bride's and groom's families. He was responsible for paying the bar tab and didn't want those other mongrels to get full bar access, so he proposed we use a code only known to his mob. Again, the booking was in jeopardy until he let go of the idea. Unbeknown to us, during the wedding night, he parked a ute in the carpark fully laden with liquor from which his group helped themselves, putting me as the licensee at extreme risk. Anyway, a year or so later, we bumped into the groom, who was working on a cattle station in the Kimberley, on the run from his new wife.

Christine made the hour-long drive down from Bomaderry every day to keep the office wheels turning and the dog fed when we were away. Our very happy association with Probus Clubs kept a steady stream of midweek group bookings coming into the lodge. We knew what they wanted because we'd taken them all over the country and stayed in all sorts of accommodation. But more importantly, we knew what annoyed them, and exorbitant bar prices topped the list. They understandably grumbled if prices were too high, and this niggle spoiled what was otherwise a very satisfactory stay. I experimented by selling a stubby for just three dollars when all others charged five to eight dollars. Instead of having one beer and bellyaching for the rest of the night, they often had three or four, then sang a few songs, told a few jokes and insisted on coming back again soon.

In the evenings we organised activities such as singalongs, card nights or movie nights. I bought a beautiful grand piano unbelievably cheaply but soon realised why. Without notice it would change tone or reverberate for no apparent reason. A piano tuner checked it over several times, but it baffled him. And it frustrated Lin, our regular singalong pianist, so much that I decided to try and fix it myself. Dressed in greasy blue overalls, I slid underneath on a mechanics floor creeper and removed the underside panels. I heard some items drop out onto the floor behind me. The problem was as simple as some children's Lego pieces rolling around inside and upsetting the pedal trap work.

Little Forest Lodge was a good fit with the buses, but after six years, we realised we needed to add more guest rooms. Some initial investigations at council revealed a likely requirement to build a large effluent treatment plant and substantial contributions towards road upgrading. Even more troubling was the real possibility we could upset our neighbours, and we didn't want to do that.

Incredibly, during this assessment period, a local real estate agent drove up with some folk from Sydney seeking a special place to establish a wellbeing retreat. They loved Little Forest Lodge and asked if we would consider selling it. My disinterested answer was that everything is for sale at a price, and I didn't give it another thought.

A week or so later, the agent rang and asked, 'Well, what is your price'? He suggested a price, and I agreed, but only if there was no haggling and messing about.

A couple of days later, before contracts were exchanged, Lindy answered a phone enquiry from someone connected with the prospective city buyers. They were discussing the proposed move to the country and wanted to know more about country life and especially about what creatures they might expect to find when living there. Lindy struggled to answer because, at that very time, I was standing on top of a chest freezer in the commercial kitchen holding a long-handled shovel and waiting for a black snake to poke its head out from underneath. She cautiously passed me the cordless phone and then stood there grinning as I answered, 'Well, I guess it's much the same here as anywhere else in the bush.'

The new owner was Mark Stephens, a celebrity meditation and hypnosis practitioner often seen on TV. He was the person who helped actress Tziporah (Kate Fischer) and radio personality Ben Fordham with their weight loss and the lodge is where he conducts seminars and retreat courses.

6
Johnny Canuck & Uncle Sam

(2005- 2009)

Hospitality burn-out worried both of us, so Lindy urged that we have some time off to enjoy each other's company without interruption. North America always held a big fascination for me, especially after our first visit there in 1982 when we drove across the country from Los Angeles to New York City, then all the way back via New Orleans. So in 2005 we went back with the intention of driving north to Alaska and see if we could learn anything about adventure tourism in that very remote part of the world.

On arrival in Vancouver, British Columbia, after the long flight, we staggered to the car rental section at the airport. To our great surprise, no rental company in Vancouver allowed their vehicles to be driven to Alaska. We were too tired to deal with the problem right then, so we caught a cab to our hotel in the city. It was summer. The sun was still up at 10:00 pm, and jetlag kept us wide awake until all hours as we contemplated how to get to Alaska. Maybe we could buy a used car just like we did twenty-three years before when we first visited the USA.

On that visit in 1982, we couldn't rent a car without giving a set time and place for its return, but on that occasion, everything worked out well after a chance meeting with a bloke involved in the car industry. We met Big Jim in a bar near San Francisco airport when he overheard our amusing conversation with a waitress. I ordered the fish of the day, but a huge square fish patty came from the kitchen.

'Are American fish square?' I asked her.

Big Jim, a large man dressed in western cowboy gear, sat nearby. He leaned over and asked with a broad southern accent, 'Are you British?'

I replied, slightly shocked because I'd never been mistaken for an Englishman before, 'No way, mate.'

'Ah, I know,' he replied with a smile, 'Aussies.'

With that he pulled up his chair, introduced himself as Jim from Odessa, Texas, and told us how much he loved getting down under ever since being there with the USAAF during WWII.

He laughed when I told him of our embarrassing introduction to America that day when I reported a blocked toilet half-full of water and lights not working to the hotel receptionist. Maybe they'd heard this before from Aussies because the receptionist mockingly answered, 'Sir, the toilet is normal, and light switches are around the other way in America.'

Jim bore a remarkable resemblance to Boss Hogg from the Dukes of Hazzard TV series, and he was amused when, after a few more beers, we started calling him Boss. He had a solution to our car dilemma.

'I'm picking you up first thing tomorrow, and we're going downtown to buy you a car,' he said. 'I saw just the car for you today when addressing a convention of car dealers.'

It turned out Jim was quite an identity in the car trade, so next morning, he picked us up in his front-wheel-drive Cadillac coupe that rode like a couch on wheels and had a bonnet as big as my Mack truck. The dealership was on the scale of Moore Park carpark on match day, and he helped our selection process by either nodding or frowning at each car we looked at. We drove away with a burnt-orange 1979 Dodge V8 coupe that accelerated like a missile but struggled to stop or go around corners. At the end of our holiday six weeks later in San Diego, Boss arranged for another dealer to buy it back for almost as much as we paid.

With that experience in the USA giving us confidence, next morning we caught a cab up to East Hastings Street—Vancouver's equivalent to Sydney's Parramatta Road. Never had I seen such junk before, but what could go wrong? By around 4:00 pm, we'd done a deal, and we drove off a lot with a black 1996 Pontiac Sunfire coupe. I was tired after a full day of pressure in the car yards and still jetlagged from the previous day, but Lindy wanted to look around Vancouver even though it was peak hour on a Friday afternoon at the start of the Canada Day holiday long weekend. I hadn't driven on the right-hand side of the road for twenty-three years and was still getting the feel of the 'Ponti'. We drove towards the city and, when approaching a busy intersection, an oncoming car turned unexpectedly across in front of us. I tried to stop, but the clutch pedal collapsed to the floor and the Ponti wouldn't stop. I wrestled the gearstick into neutral just in time to avoid a collision. Trolley buses were coming towards us from all directions and showed little patience, and car horns sounded all around. I shut off the engine, engaged low gear and jumped away on the starter motor, then managed to jump the car through the traffic to the hotel without a clutch. It was like driving 49 with its crash box and clutch-less gear shifting, but getting into the underground carpark was a little more tense. I also suspected an electrical issue because the headlights wouldn't turn off until the ignition key was off. I flipped up the bonnet and noticed an empty clutch fluid reservoir bottle but couldn't see anything obviously wrong with the electrics.

Across the street from the hotel stood a Seven Eleven store, where I bought a bottle of clutch fluid and a small shifter spanner and managed to bleed-up a good clutch pedal again with minimal effort. Then we noticed all cars driving with lights on during daylight hours, so the electrical issue feared was in fact normal operation of daytime running lights.

After several 'Buds' (Budweiser beers) that night, we both slept very soundly.

Next morning, we started out on our big Alaskan expedition by taking a route right through the city's busy downtown area. Suburban Vancouver reminded us of Melbourne with wide leafy streets and overhead wires for the trolley buses. The skyline of tall city buildings partially obscured the massive British Columbia (BC) Place football stadium, where the opening ceremony for the 2010 Winter Olympics was to be held, but the real surprise was driving along the causeway through Stanley Park with acres of parklands and large pockets of original west coast rainforest right in the city. The causeway ran out onto the Lions Gate suspension bridge, from where we got sweeping views over the harbour, city skyline and to the snow-capped mountains ahead. The magnificent Lions Gate Bridge, built in the 1930s with finance from the Guinness family of Irish stout fame, spans the first narrows of Vancouver Harbour. Two large concrete lions sit at the bridge approach, but the bridge was named after the two prominent snow-capped peaks dominating the mountain top ahead called the Lions. The impressive structure is one of

Canada's most valued national historic sites so can only be used by light vehicles.

Just beyond the bridge, we joined the famous Trans-Canada Highway for about ten minutes before it branched off towards Victoria on Vancouver Island. We then drove the spectacular Sea to Sky highway, which was undergoing major reconstruction. The narrow mountain road was being upgraded into a four-lane highway ready for the upcoming Winter Olympics, and we followed a pilot vehicle for one hundred kilometres through the roadworks up onto the Garibaldi Ranges to the ski resort town of Whistler. Everywhere we looked was a hive of summer activity, with numerous mountain-bike riders, sailors on the lakes, bushwalkers, paraglider sailors and coffee drinkers like us.

Several hours drive beyond Whistler, we reached the Cariboo Highway that we then followed for two days to Dawson Creek, 1,200 kilometres north of Vancouver. The Ponti ran like a clock and showed minimal loss of clutch fluid. We arrived at Dawson Creek on a Sunday night, so we decided to have a good rest stop before proceeding further into the wilds of Northern British Columbia. That night, while tucked up in bed, we watched the Canadian version of 60 Minutes on TV, and the feature story was about the shonky used-car business in Vancouver. The very salesman who sold us the Ponti was apparently the biggest used-car crook in the city and was accused of making numerous misleading and dishonest deals—and I thought he was quite a nice bloke.

Despite feeling a little apprehensive again about the car, we excitedly left Dawson Creek next morning to drive the famous Alaska Highway or Alcan (abbreviation of the military name Alaska—Canada Highway). We had no set plans or schedule and were relying on our *Milepost* guidebook to guide us through the 2,350 kilometres of wilderness to Delta Junction near Fairbanks,

Alaska. Ever since my school days I had wanted to make this journey after seeing the black-dotted route running through Western Canada in my atlas, and even more so after watching many documentary films about its hasty construction in WWII. When the Japanese invaded the Aleutians, their presence threatened shipping routes in the North Pacific, including those to mainland Alaska, so an overland access became imperative.

For mile after mile, the road ran through forests of spruce and lodgepole pine with a wide area kept clear of large trees either side of the road on which poplars, willow and trembling aspen thrived out in the sunlight. Often major landmarks broke the uniformity, like the mountains of the Northern Rockies and numerous lakes, rivers and muskeg bogs.

Only the occasional roadhouse or small town provided fuel and services along the highway, and very little traffic passed, other than the occasional truck, motorhome or huge pickup truck towing a fifth-wheel caravan like a small semitrailer. Our *Milepost* guidebook information made the trip interesting, especially what it told us about the historic and significant highlights along the route. I hadn't known that the road remained under military control until well after WWII and was first accessible only to civilian motorists who could satisfy a rigid permit system designed to prevent poorly prepared travellers going up there and perishing in the wilds.

The guidebook mentioned Wonowon, a small roadside service centre, at mile 101 as the last one for many miles, so we pulled up for lunch. We met a retired American couple driving their motorhome back from Alaska, asked about the road conditions up ahead and sought their suggestions on where to find somewhere to stay that night. On their advice we found the most beautiful log cabin overlooking Muncho Lake with two floatplanes moored in front ready to fly fanatical fishermen to their special places. This is where we discovered biscuits and gravy (savoury scones with white mince gravy) and Canada's gift to the world—cinnamon rolls. The further north we ventured, the more roadside cafés promoted cinnamon rolls to entice passing travellers to stop. Signs such as: Cinnamon roll and coffee $4.00; Canada's biggest cinnamon rolls; Cinnamon rolls only 99c; Cinnamon rolls family pack; World's best cinnamon rolls, and so on. I think we tried them all.

We passed maybe a dozen or more abandoned gas stations and motels scattered along the highway, built when the highway surface was gravel and no longer needed when travel became quicker once the surface was sealed. Just like along old Route 66 down in the USA, strewn around these abandoned facilities were numerous old rusty vehicle wrecks left behind from the 1950s era, when civilian traffic first had access to the highway.

We regularly saw wildlife, and the guidebook listed the animals we should watch out for when driving through the 'Serengeti of North America'—stone sheep, mountain goats, bison, moose, elk, caribou, white-tailed and mule deer, wolves, coyotes, foxes, grizzly and black bears, lynx and wolverines. We discovered that if an animal looks like a sheep, then it's a goat, and if it looks like a goat, it's a sheep. Go figure that out.

The highway surface was mostly good but changed without notice when the permafrost ground underneath warped and distorted the surface into a series of whoop do doos. If we hit those sections too fast, the little Ponti launched us from our seats almost high enough to hit our heads on the roof. We narrowly missed colliding with a gangly legged moose that stupidly darted out in front of us from where it had been hiding among the poplars, so we became much more cautious. It was easy to understand Canada's claim to have twenty per cent of all the freshwater on Earth when seeing abundantly flowing streams in every gully and many of the wider valleys filled with vast amounts of water held back by complex networks of beaver dams.

Two days after leaving Dawson Creek, we reached the wilderness city of Whitehorse built on the river flats of the Yukon River at the bottom of a wide, cliff-walled canyon, giving it a spectacular backdrop. Just upstream, the Yukon roars through a deep, narrow gorge where the foaming white water resembles the flowing mane of a white horse, hence the name Whitehorse. The town grew where the railway from Skagway met the sternwheelers plying the Yukon River during the Klondike gold rush era and later was an important base for WWII highway construction and a centre for several large Yukon mining operations. It has many claims to fame but most prized is having the freshest air of any city in the world, and the *Guinness Book of World Records* backs this up.

The population of 25,000 people swelled each day with hundreds of cruise ship passengers from Skagway enjoying short excursions from their ships or longer overland tours to Denali National Park. The historic riverfront precinct of the town was quite touristy, but not so much up on the escarpment, where most of the local commercial activity took place. We stayed at the Westmark Inn, down in the touristy part of town, because we wanted to see the Frantic Follies Show being performed at the hotel later that night. Beforehand, we strolled along the riverfront walkway beside the Yukon River, then into the Edgewater Hotel for a couple of locally brewed beers. Our first Yukon Gold was very good and the second even better. Maybe it was the water that made it better, like the Boags beer in Tasmania. We left the hotel feeling very relaxed and enjoying the frontier-town atmosphere. Whenever we got anywhere near street traffic, all vehicles travelling in either direction stopped, because in Whitehorse, pedestrians have the right of way regardless of where and how they wish to cross. A welcome change from the trauma of crossing streets in Vancouver, where it's everyone for themselves, and the cars come at you from the opposite direction to what we are accustomed.

We stumbled upon a rustic old building with a canvas-covered BBQ area emitting irresistible aromas and displaying a sign, The Klondike Rib and Salmon Bake. A charming old couple from Bismark, North Dakota, stood in the queue in front of us, and they invited us to join them for dinner. When leaving we felt as if we'd known them for years.

The Frantic Follies Show was hilarious and brilliantly presented the spirit, culture and history of the Yukon through music, poetry and vaudeville-themed live theatre. If the audience didn't understand what happened up there during the 1890s gold rush or the stern wheeler era on the Yukon, they did when leaving. A dozen banjo players on stage at once played alongside six comical musicians playing cross-cut saws with fiddlesticks. It was no wonder that all six hundred seats in the hotel function room were booked because it was so entertaining.

Our first visit to Whitehorse was one of the great highlights of our lives. We didn't know it at that point, but we would return dozens more times in subsequent years.

We decided not to continue to Fairbanks on the Alcan but divert to the site of perhaps the world's most famous gold rush at Dawson City (not to be confused with Dawson Creek). Like in Australia, driving in Canada required covering huge distances, and our diversion to Dawson City was 530 kilometres. The scenery along the North Klondike Highway was not as spectacular as on the Alaska Highway, except near the village of Carmacks, where the Yukon River ran beside the road for thirty kilometres. Carmacks had been built on the site of an old fur-trading post and later where coal was mined to fuel the sternwheelers on the river. We stopped at an elevated viewpoint to see where the river flows through the Five Fingers Rapids and where the sternwheelers once pulled themselves upstream against the current with their steam-powered winches. The anchor points were still visible on the rocks.

In the 1890s, Dawson City was the destination for 30,000 men with gold fever who risked their lives on the White Pass trail, then the treacherous six hundred kilometres journey down the Yukon River with the dream of making a fortune. A city grew very quickly where the Klondike River met the Yukon and became the capital of the Yukon Territory. The gold rush years saw many substantial buildings built, but when the gold dwindled, the government moved to Whitehorse and the city was mostly abandoned.

We strolled around the old town with its unpaved streets, timber sidewalks and many abandoned buildings, some of which leaned and twisted as the permafrost on which they'd been built had moved or melted. We thought this town must surely be a film set, but it was more like a living museum frozen in time by its isolation. The Paris of the North is still there.

Some odd things happen to people who live in isolation, especially in Dawson City where winter 'cabin fever' adds to the problem. They go a bit crazy. When we pushed through the double saloon doors into the bar at the Downtown Hotel, an old local 'sourdough' (nickname for someone who'd spent a winter up there) met us and insisted we undertake the visitors' rite of passage ritual. He filled a glass with Yukon Jack whisky and dropped a real mummified human big toe into it. We then had to drink the 'sour toe cocktail' without swallowing the toe. Lindy tried but I did not. Many years later, we heard that a young American bloke swallowed the toe as a joke, but the ritual continues with a backup toe. The toe was bequeathed to the hotel by the same sourdough we met on that first visit.

While there, we learned of a gravel road called the Dempster Highway that tracks 730 kilometres even further north to where the top of Canada meets the Arctic Ocean. We simply had to drive it. The Dempster is one of only two roads in the whole of North America crossing the Arctic Circle, the other being the Dalton Highway in Alaska—predominately a haul road to the Prudhoe Bay oilfields. Construction of the Dempster started in 1959 and opened to traffic in 1979 with the primary purpose of connecting the scattered Inuit communities to the outside world and to accommodate oil and gas exploration.

I prepared our little Ponti for the long gravel-road drive by buying a second spare wheel from a junkyard, a jerry can for extra fuel, provisions in case we got stranded by bad weather or breakdown, basic tools, spares and bear spray.

At the turn-off to the Dempster, we stopped to read the many warning signs: No emergency or breakdown services; Rough dusty surfaces with danger from flying stones; Slippery conditions; Mud and ice; Beware of large trucks; No fuel for 369 kilometres; No cell phone services; Beware of bears and so on. I was a little nervous about it because this road really was going to challenge the little Ponti and its driver, but it was just so tempting.

The north fork of the Klondike River crossing was the first point of interest followed by seventy kilometres of undulating and very slippery road conditions exaggerated by a recent heavy rain downfall. The little Ponti handled conditions quite well, especially down the long slippery hills where I kept reasonable control by using the lower gears in the manual gearbox. A roadside sign marked the entrance to the Tombstone National Park, so we pulled off the muddy road and parked, but all we could see were a couple of rough outhouses and an enclosed picnic room made from logs. Eventually we noticed an obscure, hand-painted sign pointing the way to the viewpoint, so we headed up the unmade track with no great expectations and discovered an awesome view of an immense glaciated, U-shaped valley with the jagged skyline of the Tombstone Ranges at its head, twenty kilometres away. The fringes of the valley showed where Ice Age glaciation had plucked huge slabs of rock away, leaving impressive vertical cliffs and hanging cirques. Right in front of us sat giant piles of striated terminal-moraine rocks scattered all over the wide gravel flats. If this wasn't enough, the whole lower landscape glowed purple from the fields of summer fireweed, the floral emblem of the Yukon. What a magnificent surprise!

Back on the Dempster, we climbed up and over the North Fork Pass at 4,600 feet, where a sign informed us that we were crossing the continental divide. Behind us was the watershed for the Yukon River flowing to the Bering Sea, and ahead, the waters flowed into the Arctic Ocean via the Mackenzie River. The always-shaded north faces of the mountain ranges had no vegetation, and this exposed the etched trails made by migrating caribou over countless centuries. Along the river flats were 'drunken' boreal forests of stunted black spruce trees tossed around by the freezing and thawing of the soil holding their shallow root systems. We saw a few Dall sheep licking the calcium-and-magnesium-rich rocks along creek beds, and up along distant cliffs, we saw evidence of peregrine falcon nests marked by the whitewash of droppings. At one point we came around a blind corner and found a mother grizzly standing erect on her hind legs. She exposed her teeth and razor-like claws, then ran off with her cub following closely behind.

Even after driving just two hundred kilometres, we realised that this drive was very special and possibly one of the world's most scenic roads. Our heads were hurting as we tried to absorb all the beauty of the landscape, and we commented to each other that it was like watching a National Geographic film. We even saw an elephant walking along the top of a distant ridge, but it turned out to be an eroded tor carved by nature into a lifelike elephantine shape.

Near the halfway point, I noticed a tyre on the car going flat but managed to get to Eagle Plains before needing to change it. The isolated facility had a workshop, gas station and hotel, so we thought it best to get the puncture repaired and the car refuelled before checking in to the hotel for the night. Stan, the manager of the complex, was on duty at the workshop, and he repaired the puncture, but he was much more interested to know about us. What were a couple of Australians doing right up there? And what on Earth made us think we could drive the Dempster in a little front-wheel-drive coupe? Both fair questions and the same questions we asked ourselves.

I just shrugged my shoulders and said, 'You Canucks wouldn't know a rough road even if it bit you on the bum.'

Stan enjoyed some banter and invited us to join him for a yarn later that evening. He struck me as being a very capable and practical bloke doing a mighty job to keep that complex running and providing essential services to travellers, road crews and ice road truckers. In that hostile environment, I'm sure those services could sometimes be the difference between life and death for road users.

We settled into our room at the hotel and later shouted Stan a couple of Yukon Gold beers at the bar. He introduced us to his hotel manager, Eleanor, the bar manager, Evelyn, and the house dog, Tundra, a beautiful chocolate Labrador that shadowed Stan everywhere he went. Stan told us that he'd lived up there and run the complex since its construction in 1978, just before the Dempster opened to traffic. I asked why he built it on top of an exposed ridge, and this all made sense when he explained that the site was chosen for its large area of exposed bedrock that allowed conventional construction methods, rather than building on permafrost that required deep and expensive pilings. They trucked all the fresh water from glacier creek just beyond the Arctic Circle, thirty kilometres to the north. Stan impressed us with his practical, friendly and no-nonsense approach that enabled him to survive and thrive in that harsh environment. He would've fitted in very well in the Australian outback.

Historic photos hung all along the hotel corridor walls, and two of them really intrigued me. The first was the face of a corpse belonging to the Mad Trapper of Rat River, shot dead near the hotel site in 1932 by the Royal Canadian Mounted Police (RCMP) after a dramatic seven-week manhunt through the frozen wilderness, triggered by his shooting of a police officer. Stan asked if we'd ever seen the Hollywood movie called *Death Hunt* based on that event. Apparently, it starred Charles Bronson, Lee Marvin and Angie Dickinson. The second photo of interest was that of Inspector William Dempster, who in 1911 led a search for an overdue party of Royal Northwest Mounted Police, making the regular Herschell Island–Fort MacPherson–Dawson City dog-sled patrol along the 765 kilometres route that operated from 1904 to 1921. The Dempster Highway was named after him, and it follows the land section of that route.

Stan introduced us to several truckers, one of whom ran a weekly fresh-produce service from Edmonton, Alberta, to Inuvik, Northwest Territories. A few years later, he took Scottish comedian Billy Connolly in the cab with him when filming the TV documentary *Journey to the Edge of the World*. My interest in trucks opened many conversations that night, and I enjoyed it much more than Lindy, who caught the attention of an old grader driver staying with a road-maintenance crew. The homely hotel facility and friendly staff made a comfortable and welcoming atmosphere, especially in the lounge, where many examples of taxidermy peeked at us wherever we sat. Elk, moose, sheep, Arctic fox and muskox all looked very happy to be inside where it was warm.

I must confess to being initially scared driving in the mud and ice along the Dempster because my experience was with the dust and dirt of outback Australia. It was a very different driving skill, not only due to the slippery surface but also the exaggerated camber and the road being built up very high above ground level on a thick layer of material to insulate the firm permafrost base underneath. If the permafrost ever melts, the road collapses into an impassable bog. The construction crews working on the Alaska Highway first learned this lesson in engineering. On that job they laid layers of corduroy logs over the top of the frozen ground and then covered them with gravel. However, up along the Dempster, no trees of any size grew due to the cold. The highly elevated road didn't have Armco-steel safety fencing, which would obstruct the winter snow ploughs, so I always feared slipping down off the road and overturning. It took a while to adjust to these unfamiliar conditions, but it soon became second nature.

The biggest fascination for both of us was the absence of traffic. How could it be that such an extraordinary drive was attracting less than half the traffic that braved the Peninsula Road to Cape York? The combined population of Canada and the USA was 330 million, but where were all the adventure seekers? Sure, the conditions were challenging, but still much easier than those we encountered on the drive to Cape York.

Thirty kilometres to the north of Eagle Plains, we crossed the Arctic Circle and continued for many hours until the Richardson Mountains, through which we were driving, abruptly ended at a viewpoint three thousand feet above the Mackenzie lowlands. The vast view from there stretched to the horizon over a flat landscape dotted with hundreds of small lakes scoured out over millions of years of erosion under the Ice Age Laurentide ice sheet. For the first time since leaving Dawson City, the road was dry but still needed to be driven with great caution because the surface became very loose and dusty, but much more like an Australian road.

At the Peel River, a cable ferry carried traffic across the muddy, fast-flowing river, and a bulldozer worked busily to keep the ferry approaches trafficable by pushing truckloads of ripped rock into place. I struggled getting the little Ponti aboard because of its low clearance but eventually managed to do so by driving at a sharp angle onto the ramp. The river carried many logs that appeared gnawed by beavers, and perhaps they were once part of a beaver dam washed away by heavy springtime floods. Scattered along the riverbanks were makeshift Inuit summer fishing camps with canvas walls and little smokehouses where they preserved the whitefish for winter consumption.

On the north side of the Peel River, the road became much busier, mostly with local traffic from Fort MacPherson, where we stopped briefly for our first encounter with the Inuit people of the north. The town had a bleakness and frontier feel, with unpaved and treeless streets and very modest homes, all painted the same colour. Hanging baskets of colourful flowers gave the only break from the drabness, but we guessed it would look much nicer with snow lying about for most of the year. Everyone smiled and waved at us, so we felt welcome. This town had its origin back in the days of the famous Hudson Bay Company, and I was keen to see it because I remembered seeing a TV news story when back home about how a rogue polar bear had stalked the town's residents rather than keeping to the polar ice cap like they mostly do.

Driving now was much easier and faster, and it took us just half an hour to travel sixty kilometres to the next ferry crossing over the Mackenzie River. We were unprepared for how big that river was—over a mile wide and flowing very swiftly. It drains a basin so large that only the Mississippi in North America exceeds it. As we waited for the ferry to get to us from the opposite bank, we read the signs stating that this crossing would become an ice road capable of carrying trucks weighing sixty-four tons in just two months' time. I drove aboard the large, reversible-decked, propeller-driven ferry but wondered why we headed upstream backwards rather than crossing directly over the river. The ferry operator told us that he needed to load a vehicle from the tiny village of Tsiigehtchic just up around a bend in the river. A quaint little weatherboard church with a spired bell tower marked the landing point. A big, muddy pickup truck with an all-terrain vehicle (ATV) on the back was driven aboard, carrying people dressed in camouflage hunting gear. They were heading up into the mountains for a few days of caribou hunting to stock up their winter food reserves.

Inuvik was the end point of our Dempster Highway adventure and again was a surprise because we didn't expect such a large, modern town. The town's sealed roads were buckled and rough, but the modern buildings in town were all quite straight, being erected high off the ground on pilings. A corrugated square tube running past every structure took our interest, so we asked what they were. Called utilidors, their purpose was to stop the water and sewerage systems from freezing solid by constantly circulating hot water in a pipe enclosed with them.

We booked into the Eskimo Inn Hotel for two nights and went for a walk, where we saw the most interesting church building we'd ever seen—a huge wooden structure shaped like an igloo. We bought our dinner in the nearby co-op store and noticed their wide range of stock—ammunition, groceries, fresh produce, clothing, whitegoods, hardware and even Skidoos.

Next morning, we drove to the Inuvik airport to catch a flight to Tuktoyaktuk, a traditional Inuit village fronting the Arctic Ocean. At that time, there was no summer road to 'Tuk'. The only road access was in the winter on an ice road marked out down the centre of the Mackenzie River and for fourteen kilometres out to sea before coming ashore at Tuk. They truck most of their freight from the outside world in along that winter ice road. The terminal building had a large world globe map viewed from above the North Pole, and we noticed that Inuvik was further north than the top of Iceland. The airport's huge runways allow for emergency landings of aircraft flying the north pole route and also for the operation of Canadian military aircraft. A few F-18s sat alongside the terminal building not too far from where we boarded the Twin Otter aircraft for the short flight to Tuk. On the flight we noticed down below a white Beluga whale stranded in the maze of lakes and also dozens of ice mountains or Pingoes.

Roger Gruben met us at Tuk and spent the day showing us around in his tour vehicle, a battered old yellow school bus. He even invited us back to his house for a traditional lunch of muskox soup and whale blubber. Later, he took us to an icehouse and cautiously down a ladder deep into the permafrost to where the community kept their summer catches of fish and caribou in natural frozen storage until winter. Before flying back to Inuvik, we did the obligatory Arctic Ocean toe dip by taking off our shoes and walking over the pebbled beach into the freezing water. It was so cold that it was painful just standing there long enough to get a photograph.

Tuktoyaktuk was where the 'invasion of the beer people'

stunt happened in 1995 when a beer company promoted their new 'ice-brewed beer' by holding a rock-music concert featuring the popular group Metallica.

~

A couple of days later, back in Dawson City enjoying dinner at Klondike Kate's, a nearby Australian recognised our accent. We joined Margaret's group for dinner, and conversation eventually got around to what we did for work. Her face illuminated when we told her. She worked for the Yukon Territorial Government in tourism and knew that the government was keenly wanting to assist any commercial tour operators interested in operating along the Dempster. This chance meeting opened the door for us into future commercial operations in North America. We agreed to keep in touch.

Leaving Dawson City, we drove the gravelled Top of the World Highway and entered Alaska at the isolated Poker Creek border station, then down to Haines on the coast overlooking the Inside Passage. Here, we boarded the Alaska Marine Highway System (AMHS) vehicular ferry *Matanuska* for the three-day voyage through the Inside Passage via Juneau, the Wrangell Narrows and Ketchikan to Prince Rupert, British Columbia (BC). We expected to see magnificent scenery because the Inside Passage is world famous for it, but we didn't expect the other rich sensory experiences like the smell of the fresh, salty sea air and hearing the piercing sounds made by gulls as they followed the ship. We mingled with the locals on board as the splendid scenery slipped slowly past, and we took advantage of every opportunity to get ashore whenever the vessel docked. When ashore, we strolled through isolated fishing villages just like we'd seen on TV in the John West salmon commercials. Alaska was formerly a part of Russia before the United States bought it in 1867, and even now, some of the placenames and architecture show evidence of that period. The AMHS ferry was the only vehicular link to the outside world for all those little communities and, when docked, was a hive of activity with vehicles, passengers and freight being loaded or unloaded.

At Prince Rupert, we drove off the 'Mat' feeling very rested but anxious to make the most of the remaining time before going home. We both knew our trip would be somewhat anticlimactic from here because we could never match all the thrills and experiences of the Arctic. We set a cracking pace eastward to the Canadian Rockies, then down the Ice Fields Parkway from Jasper to Banff and over the prairies past Calgary and Moose Jaw before crossing into the United States at an isolated border station between Saskatchewan and North Dakota. The US Border Officers are renowned for being intolerant to any nonsense, and we always respected this, but I reckon this time I could have been Osama himself and they wouldn't have bothered; they just wanted the beef out of our sandwiches. At that time, the US banned Canadian beef because of an isolated case of Mad Cow Disease (BSE), and North Dakota is cattle country.

In the Black Hills of South Dakota, we marvelled at Mt Rushmore and Crazy Horse Mountain sculptures before a clutch issue arose with the Ponti after it had done ten thousand trouble-free kilometres for us. The only repair workshop able to replace it quickly was in the little country town of Whitewood, sixty miles north of Mt Rushmore and just off I-90. We pulled up at the town's only motel and found a sign on the door directing guests to just choose a room and the staff would catch up later. We dropped the car at the workshop and, when walking back to the motel, saw a shed full of classic cars, including a 1960 Chrysler Imperial in Persian Sand with pink-leather seats, just like the one that Jackie Kennedy once had. We bought it and later arranged to have it shipped down to Australia. That night we went out for dinner at the truck stop over the street from the motel. The menu boasted chickens' gizzards and Rocky Mountain oysters. The only thing missing was Gomer Pyle.

Though we enjoyed our first visit to this beautiful and inspiring part of America, and as wonderful as the folks were, we found it just too touristy, busy and mainstream for our liking. Our minds and hearts were still back in the Yukon. With limited time remaining, we made a huge change of plans. From now on, no more interstate highways, just the 'blue highways', the small, forgotten, out-of-the-way roads connecting rural America—the roads drawn in blue on the old-style McNally Rand Road Atlas.

The rewards flowed thick and fast.

After leaving Whitewood, we took the overpass bridge to the north side of I-90 and followed a secondary road into Wyoming, where we noticed a large rocky outcrop shaped like an upturned bucket perhaps twenty kilometres to the west. Eventually, we got to the base of the Devil's Tower and stood there a little overwhelmed by the immense tower made up of numerous hexagonal columns rising 1,200 feet above us. We saw rock climbers high up on the columns, barely visible to us from down below, and a few hikers making the two kilometre walk around the base. There were no fast-food outlets, cheap souvenir shops or any substantial buildings for miles around. The place appealed to us, yet we'd never heard of it before.

The further we drove to the west, the more the countryside resembled the undulating hills around Gundagai in New South Wales, but the Little Bighorn River flowed between the treeless hills instead of the Murrumbidgee River. This was where General George Armstrong Custer fought his famous battle with the Plains Indians led by Chief Sitting Bull in 1876. We pulled off the road into a parking bay to see the hundreds of little white crosses scattered over the grassy landscape, each bearing the name of a soldier who died at that location. A sign warning of rattlesnakes stopped us from venturing any further.

I found the Bear Tooth Highway—a summer access road into the Yellowstone National Park from the north-eastern direction—one of the most interesting back roads because we drove to near 11,000 feet in elevation through a mountain pass between the peaks of twelve higher mountains. I'd heard reports on how non-turbo-charged diesel machines struggled to get over the pass in the thin, high-altitude air.

Cooke City (population seventy-five) stood at the top of the pass and looked like Bugtussle or Hooterville in the *Beverly Hillbillies* TV show. We needed a rest stop, but what we needed more was to track down the source of the most alluring aroma we'd ever smelled. On the porch of a small diner, we found a bloke—maybe even Jethro or Jed—barbequing ribs in a forty-four-gallon drum cut in half longitudinally and fired with hickory-wood shavings. Every few minutes he lifted the lid and basted the ribs with barbeque sauce generously dosed with Jack Daniels Tennessee whisky. Never before and never since had we eaten ribs for morning tea. A large tan-coloured bloodhound shared our gluttonous feast. He rested his wrinkly face and floppy ears on the table and appealed to us with his sunken, mournful eyes. With full mouths and sticky fingers, we smugly laughed about how good America was if you keep off the interstate highways.

It took us a while to realise that Yellowstone National Park's appeal was due more to the geothermal and wildlife highlights than the views. Even though we thoroughly enjoyed the visit, it was too crowded for us, and we were glad to get away.

Most rural towns we drove through looked as though caught

in a time warp with architecture from the early twentieth century and many with empty shops. The men wore blue jeans, flannel shirts, cowboy hats and elastic-sided boots, and when meeting us on the sidewalks, they dipped their hats and called us sir or ma'am. Typical vehicles were pickup trucks with leather gun pouches suspended behind the driver and rural supplies loaded on the back. In the little town of Waterville in Washington State, we stepped into a café and enjoyed the best milkshakes we'd ever had. The charming old lady on duty presented us with too many options, then mixed our selection with a spoon for several minutes each and served them in heavy, thick glasses much like old flower vases. She seated us in a booth with worn leather seats that probably originated in the 1940s, much like the rest of the café that still had soda fountains behind the counter and glass-framed pictures of old tractors hanging on the walls.

We ran out of time and options for backroad driving when we met I-5, just south of the Peace Arch border crossing back into Canada. It felt like the whole hectic world had closed back in around us after the peacefulness of just plodding through rural America. In Vancouver we sold the Ponti back to 'Friendly Freddie' in East Hastings Street, and a week or so later when back at home, I checked his website and saw a sales listing for our Ponti—new clutch fitted and invoices to verify.

~

Our trip served several purposes but was mainly to give us a break from the continuous grind of our busy lifestyle and constant close contact with people. Any thoughts of taking tour groups overseas weren't uppermost in our minds, although we were aware that some of our colleagues in the bus industry had done so quite successfully. But one nagging question kept me thinking about the possibility. Why weren't more people driving the Dempster Highway? Even the adventurous 4WD motorists avoided it, so I phoned Margaret, the Australian girl we met in Dawson City, and asked the question, What was it that stopped motorists from doing that drive? She answered that perhaps it was because Canadians and Americans were accustomed to driving on good roads with regular stops for food, fuel, accommodation and services, and they saw the Dempster as being much too challenging.

Apparently, school groups occasionally travelled to Inuvik by bus, and a travel company from Vancouver once took a tour group up there. Margaret gave me the contact details for the bus company in Whitehorse that operated those trips.

I couldn't stop thinking about the logistics of getting a tour group to the Yukon, so I stayed up late one night making phone calls to Canada and Alaska to piece together the possibility. Lindy was fully supportive, and we approached the planning the same as we did for any new tour. Incredibly, we both recalled hearing of a First Nations legend when in Whitehorse that warned:

'If ever you drink from the Yukon River, the waters will become part of you, and forever draw you back!'

We had, and we were. Maybe this was the driving force pulling us back?

Margaret gave us many suggestions, and we developed a draft itinerary over a few weeks of work. We presented this new itinerary in the next newsletter, and we asked for expressions of interest. Two hundred and fifty people wanted to go.

~

With great excitement in August 2006, we boarded an Air Canada 767 aircraft along with our first group of thirty-eight passengers for the long flights to Whitehorse via Honolulu and Vancouver. At Whitehorse Airport, a tired group of Australian travellers met our coach driver, JD, and his old MCI, three-axle coach with the number 828 displayed on the front windscreen—a machine remarkably similar to our old Denning Landseer number 49.

JD, a cheery French Canadian, made us all feel very welcome. After finishing a task or fulfilling a special passenger request, he often pressed a big red 'Easy' button on 828's dash, and a loud recorded voice announced, 'That was easy,' which cracked us all up. We all really enjoyed the way this francophone unintentionally mutilated the English language much like Inspector Clouseau. For example, he couldn't understand why we all erupted in raucous laughter when he apologised for the 'fogging windows'. He tried so hard to please us, even to the point of getting into a fight with an ice road trucker who unintentionally parked in our spot outside the Eagle Plain Hotel. Luckily, I saw what happened and quickly jumped in between them before they threw any punches.

However, despite how hard he tried, we soon realised that he was not a great driver, and he compensated for this by travelling very slowly. We encouraged and coaxed him where needed, but he still somehow managed to get 828 bogged right in the middle of the Dempster because he didn't know how to increase traction in slippery conditions by dumping air from the tag axle suspension to transfer weight onto the drive axle. Nor did he ever throw the slippery road air switch to disconnect the brakes on the steer axle, and this terrified me in those conditions.

**828 "bogged" on the Dempster Highway,
Northwest Territories, Canada.**

Our first international tour was quite a big deal up in the Yukon and NWT, and it made the TV news. The mayor of Inuvik even officially welcomed us to his town and formally presented each one of us with a special lapel pin.

The second Arctic tour followed a couple of days after the first one finished and was also very successful, despite it being referred to for many years afterwards in the Yukon as 'the rescued tour'.

Bruno and Christine accompanied the rescued tour over from Sydney to Whitehorse, and we were at the airport to welcome them. After a couple of days settling everyone in, we confidently waved them off with JD in 828 for their big adventure. Our plans were then to remain in North America and do some reconnaissance work on some US tours we were planning for the following year.

After farewelling them, we flew down to Vancouver, hired a big Chrysler 300 Hemi and hit the road. Friends Kevin and Stella McGrath from Oberon, who'd just done the first Arctic tour, decided to delay their flights back to Australia so they could come with us. Big Kev calculated that the extra time away from his farm in Oberon would only cost them the equivalent of about fifteen lambs.

Every night we phoned Bruno and Christine to check everything was running sweetly, and it was, until they reached Dawson City. Some very wet weather set in, so we arranged an extra night because of deteriorating road conditions up on the unsealed Dempster. Luckily, the weather cleared during their layover time, so they set off up the Dempster, aiming for Eagle Plains by nightfall.

Down in the States, we continued with our research and, as usual, that night phoned to check with them. Eleanor at Eagle Plains said that the bus hadn't arrived, and she was starting to worry. Eventually, at 10:00 pm, we received a call from Christine, who'd just reached the hotel after hitchhiking some ninety kilometres along the lonely Dempster Highway to get help. The manager Stan had only just heard gossip on the trucker's radios about a broken-down coach to the south. Christine, in tired frustration, reported that there was absolutely nothing wrong with the coach—it was the bloody driver.

Apparently, JD suffered an anxiety attack and refused to go any further even though the road was open and trucks were cautiously passing by.

Stan arranged for a rescue party to go down and drive the coach up to Eagle Plains. It wasn't all bad, though, for the passengers stranded on the coach, because while they waited for rescue, the northern lights put on quite a spectacle, a grizzly bear with cubs strolled by and Bruno, the former singing barman, entertained them. Eventually, they made it to Eagle where they were warmly welcomed and looked after very caringly.

The coach company in Whitehorse acted quickly to get a replacement driver up to Eagle Plains, some 850 kilometres to the north, and by about 3:00 pm the next day, the replacement driver, Donna, arrived to find the group in very high spirits and happy to head off right away. They loaded the coach without delay, and it pulled away to a loud cheer. After several hundred metres, however, it came to a grinding halt and rapidly reversed back because Donna had forgotten something.

A passenger down the back exclaimed, 'She goes faster backwards than JD did forwards.'

Donna, a grandmother in her sixties and a native Yukoner, was very confident driving in those conditions, and she brought the tour back with happy travellers. Some years later she came to Australia with husband Ken and did an outback trip with us.

While the rescue effort was happening up in the Yukon, news broke in the outside world about the death of the Crocodile Hunter, Steve Irwin. We were in a bar in Billings, Montana, till very late that night using their payphone to direct the rescue effort and get the tour back on track. During this time, quite a few Americans came over to us and expressed their sadness as if we had known him personally.

With the Arctic tour back underway, we continued with our reconnaissance trip down in the States. Big Kev and Stella were great travel companions, and we often laughed at Kev's humour when he equated most spending with how many lambs or cuts of lamb things cost. For example, a nice dinner for the four of us would cost about two kilograms of chops plus a leg of mutton.

Several weeks after getting home, word had spread around

from returning passengers that the Arctic trip was something very special, and Christine started getting many more enquiries with some even coming from New Zealand, England and Canada.

~

The second year in Canada got off to a sad start. We held a booking from an elderly but spritely lady living alone at Mollymook, not far from where we lived at Little Forest. We were concerned about how she would handle the long flights, so we encouraged her to travel up to Sydney with us on the afternoon prior to the departure date and booked her at the same hotel near the airport. When we called to pick her up, she was busily vacuuming the floors and explained that if for any reason she didn't make it home, she didn't want people going through her possessions and thinking she was untidy. Very sadly, she didn't make it home after suffering a severe stroke on the first night in Whitehorse.

It wasn't a great start, but the group expressed their wish to push on and enjoy the tour to the fullest. Luckily, we had Lionel and Dawn Boxsell from Nowra travelling with us, who were good friends of our parents. Dawn had longed to visit Alaska ever since they hosted an Alaskan Rotary Exchange student, and she was so excited that when she stepped on Alaskan soil for the first time, she bottled the soil and brought it home.

Lionel came to the group's rescue one night at our hotel in Beaver Creek on the Alaska Highway. Several hundred international cruise ship passengers in transit by coach from Skagway to Denali National Park also stayed at the hotel. During dinner we learned that each group was expected to perform something afterwards, so Lionel led us in a brilliant impromptu rendition of 'Waltzing Matilda', and we won the prize for the best performance.

A few weeks later, we returned to Beaver Creek with the next tour group, well prepared, this time, for our performance under the guidance of a retired music teacher travelling with us. We gave such a polished rendition of 'Waltzing Matilda' that the other groups thought we were a choir and grumbled that it wasn't fair.

~

For another three years we used 828 and continued our learning process about doing business overseas and organising and managing large groups of travellers from Australia. We also chartered coaches elsewhere in the US but, even though they were acceptable, we never found the operator we hoped to find. On one occasion we chartered a coach and guide from Vancouver for an eighteen-day tour into the States, and though when in Canada, the guide was fantastic, down in the States, he was uninterested because he didn't like Americans or America. With another operator out of Dallas, Texas, we had a driver who only wanted to drive point to point via the quickest route, so we fought daily battles to get to go the way we wanted.

I took responsibility for all the operational issues and tour commentaries, while Lindy looked after the passengers' welfare. The first tour of 2008 challenged both of us simultaneously when we transitioned a group through Vancouver Airport. A married couple lost their passports and airline officials denied them passage on their connecting flight to Whitehorse. With little time to sort it out, Lindy gave them reassurance, a photocopy of their passports from her files and re-booked their flights for the following day while I arranged a hotel, taxi and contact details for the Australian Consulate in Vancouver. We had no choice other than to leave them behind in a city they'd never been to before and hoped they could sort it all out and catch up with us in Whitehorse the next day.

Late afternoon on the following day, we met the weary couple again as they checked into the hotel in Whitehorse. The receptionist asked for ID and, without hesitating, the husband reached into his inside jacket pocket and produced the two original passports that had been in his pocket the whole time. His wife barely spoke to him for about a week before beginning to see the funny side.

After four busy seasons, we still had a steady demand for seats on Arctic tours, but we became quite concerned about 828, the old MCI coach we'd been chartering. In many ways it was ideal because it was a strong old thing with no electronics. (Does that sound familiar?) It belonged to the huge cruise ship company Holland America based over the border in Fairbanks, Alaska, and often looked neglected. Before each season I donned overalls and spent several hours inspecting it and making a list of things that needed attention before taking it up into the wilds where we had limited support. Often, the list would include the most basic things like having a spare wheel and tools to change it with along with mechanical issues needing attention. I also carried a satellite phone brought over from Australia because the coach only had a VHF radio suitable for vehicle-to-vehicle communications.

Worse, we had safety concerns following several alarming events. One happened when coming down the steep two-mile descent from the Midnight Dome Mountain behind Dawson City. The driver unknowingly applied the Jacob Brake (engine compression brake) without the Allison transmission being locked up, then, with no effective engine braking, rode the service brakes all the way to the bottom with burning smell and smoke wafting throughout the bus. It was extremely dangerous!

We thought about the possibility of owning and operating our own bus for a year or so and had already made a trip down to Seattle to look at some used machines, but I couldn't find anything suitable. Also I spent hours studying all the Canadian and US bus operator compliance requirements.

On many occasions I heard Australian businessmen say that if you can do business in Australia with its endless rules and regulations, then it will be a breeze in North America.

We both knew that by committing to a new vehicle over there, we would need to spend much more time away from Australia. The alternative was to keep doing what we'd been doing for the last fifteen winters—bashing ourselves and equipment endlessly running up to Cape York and back.

Touring in the Yukon had become a delightful part of our lives, and we loved sharing it with all our passengers. We wanted to do it—so we did.

7
MAN's Redemption;
Bus Number Three

(2006, four years earlier)

After our first MAN bus clocked up 400,000 kilometres, we replaced it with another mechanically quite similar machine, but this one had a body built by Coach Design.

Lindy and I had just arrived back from our exploratory trip to Canada and really loved the business again. I felt much more at ease and didn't take on any more work than we could handle. We scaled back to a one-bus operation and only did the job because we wanted to, not because we needed to. Also, from then on, we only ever toured to the places to which we loved going.

With Little Forest Lodge sold, we moved to Cambewarra, quite close to where we lived before moving to Milton. The house on five acres nestled in below Mt Cambewarra with a beautiful spring-fed creek flowing through the property. The views were almost as good as those from Little Forest Lodge, but we looked up at the mountain rather than down from it.

We set up an office in a room at the front of the house, and with the doors open onto the veranda, we enjoyed the tranquil sound of water flowing in the creek and birds singing in the trees. It was very convenient—or too convenient—especially when we started running tours to North America, which made much of our office work happen through the night due to time-zone differences.

By 2006, we generated sufficient business without needing to advertise, and many of our regular passengers toured with us ten to twenty or more times. They became more like friends rather than customers, and we looked forward to having them with us each time.

~

Some amusing things happened, and we enjoyed hearing our regulars recalling them.

One Friday night we had a large group in the Catholic Club at Coffs Harbour for dinner, and not knowing how long to allow, I told them all to listen for an announcement saying what time the bus would leave. When our departure announcement came over the Club's PA system, it brought panic to many good Catholics there that night: 'The Bishop's bus will depart in ten minutes.'

Another story people often recalled indicated how I should try to be a bit clearer when asking for help. While loading a group in Forster, passengers trying to get on the bus and others trying to get off created a jam at the steps. I asked a lady to get out and stop the traffic so that those on the bus could get out. No one told me she was a recently retired police officer. She strode out into the middle of the highway behind the bus and brought all the traffic to a standstill. Several weeks after getting home I received the following report of the incident from her in the mail, although there are discrepancies between her version and mine:

> *Stop the Traffic*
>
> *Bruce, our captain, was helping a passenger up the bus steps. He turned to me and said, 'Will you stop the traffic until I get out, please?' Sure, I thought, apparently it wasn't the best parking spot, so off I trotted to stand in readiness at the back of the bus for my captain's signal to 'Stop the traffic.' I had no qualms about doing this being an ex-copper, but I did wonder how he had discovered I was so trained.*
>
> *As the stragglers got on the bus, a worrying thought passed my mind. How was I to stop the traffic and still get on the bus? Back to the captain I trolled. I put my dilemma to the captain, who looked at me dumbfounded. In anguish, Bruce said 'You stopped the traffic!! I wanted you to stop the passengers so I could get off the bus!'*
>
> *'Well,' I said in shocked astonishment, 'I have never heard of people called traffic before!' Rodney, a passenger, was waiting to board the bus. I approached him and in my most ex-official voice said to him, 'You are traffic. You are to keep within the speed limit and not overtake on the near side.' I boarded the bus having satisfied myself I had carried out my duties.*
>
> *Signed by an unnamed ex-copper on the great Gloucester trip.*

What are the chances of having two ladies with the same names on consecutive tours? On the first tour, Wendy Davis travelled with husband Graham. They extended for an extra night at the hotel in Adelaide following the tour so Wendy could catch a day trip to Kangaroo Island. Graham stayed back at the hotel and arranged for a room change during the day without telling Wendy. When she returned late that night, her room card wouldn't open the door, so she went to reception and asked for a recoded door card. They gave her a coded card to the room of the second Wendy Davis, who'd booked in early for the next tour. When the door opened, the two Wendys faced off. Their awkward encounter took them some time to sort out!

I enjoyed the evenings most on the outback camping tours. At the end of a long day, it was good to sip a cold beer while helping Lindy prepare dinner and to mingle with the passengers. After a week or so of these casual evenings, we all became familiar enough for a little banter to break out. I cringe as I recall the time a lady asked me where the saltshaker was during dinner.

I pointed to it right in front of her and stupidly said, 'If it was a snake, it would've bitten you.'

She reacted with horror—unusual for an offhand remark— and afterwards, her travelling friend told me that her husband died when a snake bit him while he walked through a paddock on his rice farm.

After a few days on tour, some passengers opened up more than others and told us way too much. Sometimes this could be embarrassing, especially if we were stranded with them. One morning I was busily cooking a small mountain of toast and harmlessly said to a passenger, 'How are you this morning?'

The answer took five painful minutes. From sleep habits to joint replacements, medications, hospitalisations and so on, but when he disclosed his haemorrhoidal issues, I vowed never to ask that question again. From then on, it was always, 'Great day today, isn't it?'

Occasionally we found ourselves in awkward situations, like when we discovered that a partially disabled lady who sought help with most activities, especially from her long-suffering but loyal husband, was a fraud. I watched her struggle around a corner by herself to where she thought she was out of sight, then saw her pick up her walking frame and run like an athlete to be first at the shops.

~

We'd just driven over McKillops Bridge spanning the Snowy River and followed a narrow mountain road similar to what you'd expect to find in the Andes in Bolivia, when my mother-in-law created another awkward situation by giving me an unambiguous directive. 'You'll never go that way again, will you, Bruce?'

And I haven't!

~

We operated each outback camping tour with the security of knowing that the Royal Flying Doctor Service (RFDS) was just a satellite phone call away. On two very sad occasions, we needed to use their services, and this encouraged us to promote every opportunity to contribute to their needs. Our groups donated profits from the drink box for many years, and the tally eventually exceeded $100,000. A fair contribution towards this came from the millionaire's trip, when a group of wealthy passengers loaded half a ton of quality wines and craft beers in Broome and dispensed it at a healthy mark-up. Their contribution was triple the next highest tally.

On Cape York tours, we supported the Vietnam Veterans, who had a permanent camp near Kalpowar Crossing, and funding for the Long Tan Memorial at Morton Telegraph Station near the Wenlock River crossing.

Bus number three crossing the Jardine River on the Cape York tour.

Behind bus number three, we towed a new trailer equipped with toilets for use whenever we stopped alongside the road where other facilities weren't available. After such a stop, just before departure, I normally started the bus to signal time to go, then I got out and walked behind to close the trailer doors and turn off the water pump to the handbasins. Being an opportunist, I also popped inside the trailer to use the facility myself. One day, a helpful passenger walked past and, hearing the engine running, thought I'd forgotten to close the trailer, so he locked the doors from outside, trapping me. No one could hear my calls for help, but after a search for the missing driver, they eventually found and rescued me.

While camped at Carnarvon Gorge in central Queensland, Ken Douglas got stuck in the trailer when the latch broke after corrugated roads shook it to bits. He popped into the loo and latched the door during an evening singalong led by a passenger with a compact keyboard. I heard his calls for help, so I got my toolbox from the bus and started dismantling the lock to free him. This created interest and amusement, encouraging the group to sing with gusto, 'Oh dear, what can the matter be? Ken D's locked in the lavatory …'

The trailer toilet system was the same as on a coach, but it was important for users to understand the one big drawback. Rather than hang instructions on the wall, we attached the following poem:

> *SPECIAL REQUEST*
> *I seek your help to stop the problem I will tell*
> *Caused by thoughtless actions that can cause a maintenance hell!*
> *To place foreign objects in the item on which you sit*
> *Can block the mechanism's pump, that pumps away the ----*
> *A rubber glove must then be placed upon a wary bloke*
> *Who then must delve to deep within, to unblock the pipes that choke.*
> *So just remember that the job that's dreaded most,*
> *Is done by the very hand of he who cooks your breakfast toast!*

Bruno crewed with us every year during his annual holiday break from TAFE and Christine sometimes joined him. At night around the campfire, he often told of his travels, particularly to the Corletto ancestral homeland in the northern Italian Alps. He always spoke with such passion that many urged him to take tours over to Italy. Lindy and I felt indebted to Bruno and Christine for their many years of loyal help and friendship, so we also urged them to have a go at leading their own tours. We offered to help in any way they needed, but Christine already knew how to do all the arrangements because she'd been doing ours for years. In 2014 they led their first highly successful tour. After a year or so, Bruno resigned from TAFE to pursue the tour business further and to work more with us. He became our main Bigfoot and support-truck driver, and we covered for each other when either of us were overseas.

Bruno and Christine in the Italian Alps, 2015.

Life on the road was good to us, and despite many challenges, we had a terrific time and especially enjoyed treating our support crews to nights out on special occasions or whenever we could. Crewmember Denis celebrated his sixtieth birthday at Coral Bay in Western Australia, so we had a special night for him and gave him a joy flight in a motorised hang-glider as his birthday present. Next morning, I drove him out to the airstrip and watched the rickety flying machine take off. While I waited, the publican, who we'd met the previous night, asked for my help to push his aircraft out of a hanger. It was like a fancy little twin-seat sportscar, and I was very impressed. He asked if I'd like to go for a fly with him, and within no time at all, we were up in the air over Coral Bay. We whooshed past poor Denis and proceeded to loop the loop and do some barrel rolls. Meanwhile, Lindy was in camp preparing lunch for the group, and they all commented on that crazy fool up in the air overhead.

Several days later on that tour, we were snapped back to reality. After a good day on the road, we pulled up at our Bush Lodge camp set-up at Eighty Mile Beach in Western Australia. Everything appeared normal. I asked Denis how his day had been and was surprised at his answer—it was possibly the worst day of his life. A distracted driver ran him off the road and smashed the truck over a rocky outcrop. The top of the truck looked undamaged, but underneath was a total write-off. A grader driver saw what happened and towed it to that night's campsite.

The next day we had it trucked 250 kilometres into Broome and set up camp overlooking Roebuck Bay. Luckily, we had three days scheduled in Broome and were able to buy an almost-identical new truck and swap the bodies over.

Trouble one time came from the most unlikely source—a national parks ranger. Denis and his crew of two German backpackers arrived at Windjana Gorge with the support truck and began erecting the camp. Not long after this, a ranger confronted them.

'Where are your name badges?' he demanded.

'We don't have any,' Denis replied courteously.

'Then how do I know you're commercial operators and entitled to set up here?' He got back in his vehicle, and before driving away, threatened them with, 'I'll be back later, and you better be wearing badges.'

Several hours later I arrived in camp with the bus group, and

Denis told of his encounter. We hatched a plan aimed at making a joke of the unreasonable threat. Lindy gave each crewmember and passenger a cardboard dinner plate and asked them to write their names on the plates with a thick felt pen and then pin them to their shirts, making the world's biggest name badges.

During dinner, the ranger's vehicle approached, this time driven by a different ranger. Seeing the giant name badges everyone wore, he suspected we'd gone nuts and, with a grin, asked what was going on. When told of his colleague's unusual behaviour, he laughed hard and said, 'Don't worry, it's just a Vietnam thing he's got going on.'

We all relaxed after that and enjoyed another typical Kimberley sunset as the sheer limestone cliffs of the Windjana Gorge glowed with such colour they could've been lit from within. All this beauty hid the macabre history of this site, where in 1894 thirty armed police fought Aboriginals led by Pigeon/Jandamarra. The Battle of Windjana Gorge elevated Pigeon/Jandamarra's legend to immortal status among the tribe.

In the busy years, we had far more trouble with the support truck than the bus, mostly because our seasonal crews didn't have much experience driving in harsh conditions. We dealt with a bent chassis, accident damage, broken springs, burnt brakes, contaminated fuel, smashed radiators, cooked engines, equipment lost from unlatched doors, overhead tree damage, blown tyres, snapped axles, smashed rear-view mirrors and so on.

All tour operators working in the harsh outback conditions had trouble from time to time, and most of us would give each other assistance if we could, knowing that our time would come one day. The public also saw us as a source of emergency help, whether it be for satellite phone use, tools to borrow, mechanical repairs, towing, using items from the first aid kit or information on road conditions.

An unknown driver put us to the test on Cape York when his small Suzuki 4WD overturned and skidded past the bus on its side. We sprang to action, hauled the driver out of the vehicle and rendered first aid. As he settled down, a few of the men on the bus tipped the Suzuki back onto its wheels and managed to get it started. Though dazed, the driver still intended to continue with his trip to the top of the Cape. We urged him not to and convinced him to turn around, so we could follow him back to Musgrave Station and give help if needed. Incredibly, he took off like a madman, and when we got to Musgrave, there was no sign of him. I asked if he'd called in and was told that he'd stopped to refuel, then left in a great hurry without paying.

Only on rare occasions did we have any unpleasant issues with other tour operators, and if we did, it was mostly from the parochial small local ones when young blokes were starting out in the tour business. If they survived for more than a season or two, they settled down and became part of the tour-industry family. The two biggest operators in Australia were a different story, however. Locked into intense competition with each other, they were wary about giving away operational secrets, and we suspected they were both watching us. A simple, poorly presented fellow booked on one of our Kimberley tours and became a nuisance, getting underfoot and asking dozens of unusual questions about all aspects of our operation. We didn't take him too seriously, thinking he was just a bit different, but after the tour, at the Alice Springs Airport, Bruno and I saw the same man sitting in the Qantas lounge dressed in an expensive suit and reading the *Financial Review*. Later that season, a driver from one of the big companies seemed excited to meet us and talked about how his company used our operation to benchmark their staff training. I didn't think to ask if the benchmarks were for how well we did things or how poorly.

Luckily, we weren't competing with either of them, and we couldn't be block booked out of key locations, like they tried to do to each other, because we used the mobile Bush Lodge camp.

Only a few months after taking delivery of bus number three, we were touring in the Pilbara region of Western Australia. We'd had the new bus sign written in a hurry before leaving home and it had a spelling mistake—Blue Moutains instead of Blue Mountains—on the side that people seldom noticed because of the very small letters. Except at the Hamersley Gorge Visitors' Centre. While Lindy led the group inside the centre, I took a little shut-eye in the bus with my seat laid back, so people walking past couldn't see me. An old Coaster bus pulled up nearby, and a cocky young tour guide got out and unloaded his small group of European backpackers. He gathered all his group to the side of my beautiful new bus and proceeded to make quite a big deal about the spelling mistake.

My first impulse was to jump out and confront him but wisely chose not to. When they eventually went inside the visitors' centre, I got out and spent fifteen minutes closely inspecting his old bus. If I could find a fault, I planned to embarrass him in front of his group. I even scrambled underneath it, hoping to find something, but couldn't find a single thing wrong.

Later in the day, we met up again at one of the walking-track access points. I couldn't believe my luck when I noticed something I hadn't noticed before. The sign written on the side of his bus—Beyond Your Expectations—had inverted commas around it. I sat and waited for his group to return, then beckoned them over to the side of his bus and pointed out how wrong it was to capitalise the three words in the inverted commas. I then smugly explained to his group how my brand-new bus had been hurriedly prepared for the season while his old bus had been wrong for at least twenty years.

Whenever issues confronted us, we had a head start on many operators because Christine, back in the office, took care of things. For example, she found and booked motel accommodation and meals for forty people in less than an hour when we learned that bankruptcy receivers had just closed the motel at which we were to stay that night. In Tasmania on one occasion, a dispute arose between the owners of a motel and the adjoining restaurant where we had group bookings for four consecutive tours. The motel owner threatened that if we utilised the restaurant next door, he'd kick us out of his motel, so Christine made alternative arrangements at short notice. And, when Ansett Airlines collapsed, she assisted dozens of passengers with arrangements to get home.

In the days before online bookings and interactive websites with FAQs and other information, Christine answered every letter personally. One lady sent a letter of complaint at being awarded the 'Bunny of the day' title for doing something silly that required her to wear bunny ears all day in the bus. This happened on a trip operated by our good friends Paul and Barbara Burgess when doing a quick shuttle run for us out to Broken Hill. When Christine phoned Lindy for advice, they both got the giggles but still managed to agree on a diplomatic answer. Many years later I was laughing about this event among a group of passengers who, all except one, thought it was funny. The one who didn't think it was funny was the one who made the complaint. (Judy, I'm still sorry about that.)

Sometimes, back home in the office, Christine dealt with issues without us even knowing about them. Like the time she had a call from an irate Bazza in Leonora, Western Australia, accusing us of stealing his firewood. He phoned our office and threatened Christine that, if the wood wasn't returned by that afternoon along with a 'slab of piss', he was going to call the cops. Christine rang Denis in the support truck because we weren't answering the phone in the bus. Denis told her that we hadn't taken the wood; 'Spinach Man' had taken it.

Reaching her breaking point, with a raised voice, she demanded, 'What is going on out there? Have you all gone mad? Who the hell is the Spinach Man?'

The cause of all the trouble was quite innocent. While walking through a side street in Leonora, some of our group spotted a vegetable garden with the best spinach they'd ever seen. The owner got into a yarn with them and promised to bring some over for dinner. Lindy gratefully invited him to stay and join us. It was a cold night, so he borrowed some wood for our campfire from his mate Bazza, who lived in a caravan beside our campsite. Bazza wasn't home at the time; he was down at the pub. After dinner I delivered my usual evening announcements to constant interjection from our dinner guest—whose name I had forgotten.

Eventually, I bluntly said, 'Now listen here, Spinach Man, a bunch of spinach can only buy you so much slack. How about you shut up for a while?'

The group roared with laughter, then started calling him Spinach Man. He forgot to tell Bazza about the wood.

Problems and challenges made life interesting out on the road. Even the most harmless things like pulling up in a roadside rest area for morning tea could become tense. South of Derby in Western Australia we stopped for a cuppa and, shortly after, so did a really mean-looking bikie on his big Harley. Bearded, tattooed and pierced all over, he approached the group with a snarl on his face and gruffly asked me for a loan of a fourteen-millimetre spanner.

His bizarre request shocked me, and without considering the consequences, I stupidly replied, 'You mean a nine-sixteenth, mate.'

His attitude then became like that of a dog with its tail between its legs, because he knew how preposterous it was for any true Harley rider to think anything metric for a classic American motorcycle.

Mostly our modest operation caused interest and compliments, especially from the 'grey nomads' or retirees with caravans who closely watched activities in our camp. Sometimes their curiosity got the better of them and someone would come over to see what was cooking for dinner or what people were discussing.

Lindy had meticulous catering hygiene procedures. She'd completed several training courses and had consulted with experts, who all advised her to use disposable plates in the absence of a commercial dishwasher. She didn't like doing it, and it cost us a fortune, but we had no choice. When this information reached the nomads at one campsite, a lady travelling alone in a Kombi camper covered in ban-the-bomb stickers overheard something and stormed into our camp ranting about everything from seals to icebergs. She demanded I give her the address of my boss so she could chew his ears off as well. I wrote it on a piece of paper. She exploded—figuratively speaking—when she noticed that the address I'd given her was exactly where she was standing. I introduced myself to her as the boss.

Luggage was another great source of amusement for us. What people packed constantly bewildered us. A lady with the heaviest case ever wore the same clothes every day, while others turned up with musical instruments, tools for every need, bottles of home brew, garden gnomes and once, even a full clown suit. But I always knew when someone had bottles of scotch in their bag because they always gave specific instructions on how to load them into the bus—'Bruce, this bag must always be carried this way up.'

Luggage also caused issues for us in the mornings because passengers never seemed to know where to leave their bags ready for the crew to load them into the bus, despite how many times we told them. Passengers dropped luggage on both sides of the bus or even so close to the luggage door that we couldn't walk over it or around it to get to the door. But mostly they just dropped it where the first bag landed, no matter where that was. Eventually, I had a brainwave; lay out a blue tarp on the ground for them to place their bags on. This failed badly one morning when a nearby bus group also laid out their blue tarp. We had to separate the mixed luggage even though the buses were thirty metres apart. Apparently, the other bus operator had the same luggage issues as us.

The morning routine saw the crew grab an early bite of breakfast on the run so they could pack the camp away while everyone else ate, but we always had one or two passengers who never slept and prowled the camp all through the night. It didn't matter how early we got to breakfast, these insomniacs were already there wanting to join us. They wanted their full breakfast early, and this disrupted ours and gave them more time to hassle those making a later start. For years we tried to cater for them but found there was simply no end to the problem. If we had breakfast at 6:00 am one day, they wanted it at 5:30 am next day and so on. After about twenty years of this, I cracked and set breakfast times in stone and with just one sitting. It worked okay but created another issue—the early birds encircled the crew like sharks as we ate.

Most people enjoyed the evenings, especially after having a few drinks and enjoying another one of Lindy's great meals. After dinner we held the evening announcements session to give information on the following day, answer any questions and to have some fun. Sometimes it took five minutes, and other nights it went on for hours, depending on how lively the groups were. We always made time for people with fascinating stories or singers, musicians and joke tellers, but what I dreaded most was listening to poorly written poetry—unless it was so bad it was funny—but we still clapped graciously.

On some perfect starry nights, we enjoyed open-air cinema using the back of the trailer as a screen. On these memorable nights, Lindy always seemed to find special nibblies and hot chocolate at intermission. In later years we acquired a satellite dish mounted on a tripod stand and tuned into special events like the State of Origin footy games. All the cheering coming from our campsite often attracted quite a crowd. One such night on Mabel Downs Station in the Kimberley near the Bungle Bungles, we soon had a crowd of near sixty rowdy Queenslanders and New South Welshmen enjoying the tussle. At half-time during a quick exodus for the facilities, someone tripped over the cable to the satellite dish and the screen went dead. I couldn't fix the damage so tuned the AM radio to the only station clear enough to listen to. Problem was, we had no idea what was happening because the commentators were rampaging Roy Slaven and HG Nelson and, as entertaining as it was, I had to make regular satellite phone calls to keep the score updated.

Nothing brought more fun than baiting the AFL fans, but I never let on how much I admired their passion. They are the ultimate fans, on the same level as the supporters of the New

Zealand All Blacks. However, State of Origin nights always left them a little bewildered and feeling left out. I quickly picked the easiest ones to provoke because they were first on the defensive and asking to watch 'real' football. At Fitzroy Crossing on one of these nights, for no other reason than the word 'Fitzroy' being in the name of the place, the handful of Victorians sang, 'We are the boys from ol' Fitzroy (me lads) … Carn the Roys!'

One weekend towards finals time, we were out of radio range, so I made a satellite call to get all the weekend results to relay to the passengers on Monday morning. I delivered the NRL scores, followed by super rugby and soccer before the inevitable cry from down the back from Pete the farmer from Swifts Creek, 'What about the real football?'

'Oh mate, didn't you hear the big kerfuffle?' I said with fake sympathy. 'All the AFL games were cancelled last weekend. I'm surprised you didn't know.'

'What?' he spluttered in shocked disbelief. 'Why?'

'Lack of interest, mate,' I replied smugly.

At the start of most tours, many passengers strung clothesline ropes from tent to trees or between tents when first arriving at camp. This seemed harmless enough, but within minutes, a trail of green ants started marching from the trees into all the tents connected by rope. And, of course, the camp became an obstacle course in the dark, threatening to decapitate unwary walkers. It took a while to train each group into a smooth team operation and mostly we reached that point just in time to bid them farewell.

We still feel guilty when thinking of some of the situations we put our poor passengers into, like the night near Giles weather station, 350 kilometres west of Uluru. The howls of dingoes filled the clear, still night for hours after bedtime before they invaded the camp, scattering plastic containers, buckets and utensils around for several hundred metres. A little helper turned up, a Jack Russell bitser, who patrolled all night for us, and next morning at breakfast, I told him what a good boy he was. I'm certain he knew what I said because he gave a hint of a head wobble. That night was so cold that next morning we had to whack the tents with the back of a shovel to break off the ice.

Occasionally, we did terrible things to passengers who deserved it, like to an old rugby teammate being deliberately recalcitrant. On the last morning of the tour, when he wasn't looking, Bruno helped me put a heavy rock into his suitcase. It took both of us to lift it into the luggage bin. That night when dropping him at his Cairns hotel, he couldn't budge his case off the ground.

Often, we saw people who reminded us of someone, or passengers told us we reminded them of somebody. A passenger hounded me for days about how he recognised me from somewhere, so eventually I thought I'd be funny and said that perhaps he knew me from when I was a warder at Long Bay Jail. He seemed to avoid me after that.

Late one night we headed down the coast for home after dropping a group back in Sydney and were pushing hard to beat my approaching eight-hour compulsory driver rest break. Just south of Kiama is a stretch of very windy road known as the Kiama bends, and it's notorious for causing car sickness. Don't be disgusted, dear reader, but driving a loaded coach around these corners requires the same skill as with a truckload of cattle—steady and smooth. But with no passengers aboard this late night, I launched into the corners much like I did when 'flying' the Mack through 'The Aeroplane' years before.

I knew this road well and recalled racing along it on my way to under-fourteen-years football training while hanging on in the back seat of a Mini Cooper S police car driven by my policeman coach. Lindy startled me with a slap on the shoulder, saying, 'Have you forgotten we still have two ladies aboard?' Alarmingly, I had. In the rear-view mirror, I saw arms and legs everywhere but also two huge grins.

In Tasmania, in order to see the tallest hardwood trees in the world and the site of many well-publicised logging disputes at the Valley of the Giants, we had to drive along a forestry track with several log bridges. We'd been there many times without any issue, but one time a flood-damaged bridge displayed a newly erected load-limit sign indicating that our bus was too heavy to cross fully loaded, so I asked the passengers to walk over the bridge and I followed behind with the empty bus. When they were halfway over, I agonised over whether to mention that they were crossing the Styx River. (In Greek mythology the Styx River is the border between the world of the living and the afterlife. To cross over successfully required paying the ferryman, which is why they buried people with a coin under their tongue—for the fare.)

Have you ever had a bad day? Our bad day should've been a simple five-hour run along a gravel highway from Innamincka to Thargomindah with a stop at the historic Dig Tree of Burke and Wills fame. Things started to go wrong when we got to Cooper Creek and found that recent flooding had left the road impassable for our eighteen-ton vehicle. The publican at Innamincka told us of a possible detour, but when we got to a concrete causeway along that route, we found it also flood-affected and covered in deep, soft sand. Already anxious about how late we were, I risked the crossing only to make it halfway before grinding to a halt in the deep sand. Miraculously, we managed to reverse back out of trouble even with the four-ton trailer behind. The group was quite stressed, so we stopped there on the creek bank for an early lunch while we all settled down.

One of the passengers was celebrating a birthday, so Lindy went to a side bin of the bus, stuck some sparklers into a fruit cake and lit them. We all sang 'Happy Birthday' but before finishing someone yelled, 'Fire!' Some items in the side bin had caught fire from the sparklers. Luckily, we extinguished it quickly, but then one of the passengers told me he needed to get medication out of his suitcase buried at the very bottom of the trailer, so I manhandled all the luggage out, then put it all back in.

A long detour took us almost back to the Warry gate on the Queensland/New South Wales border, so when we arrived at Noccundra after dark, we found the fuel supplier closed. I dipped the tank with a stick and realised we'd be very lucky to reach Thargomindah. Though by then it was about 10:00 pm, we had no other option than to try. When the lights of Thargomindah finally came into view ahead, the engine started to miss, so I swerved from side to side to slosh the remaining fuel into the pickup tube. This got the bus just several kilometres from town before it stopped. The local school bus operator rescued us, and while the group ate dinner at midnight, I delivered luggage to the caravan park, hotel and motel using a borrowed ute. Then I took a jerry can of fuel back to the bus and worked for another hour to bleed the fuel system.

Three weeks later, when back in Thargomindah with the next tour, I had a phone call around four in the afternoon from a passenger from the previous trip, who knew we'd be back there at that time. He asked how we were travelling, and I was happy to report the group was already at the pub enjoying a cold beer.

Even though we had our lives scheduled two years in advance, sometimes the goalposts shifted like on that bad day, but what terrorised me most was the possibility of being stranded out on the Tanami Track running one thousand kilometres through the Tanami Desert between Halls Creek and Alice Springs during or after rain. Before each crossing I watched the weather forecasts for days without fail, especially in late April or early May when late monsoonal deluges were possible. Even a single storm could turn the road into a soft, sticky, slippery mess and make previously dry creek beds run with deep, red muddy water. Once committed to a crossing, there was no turning back or any support. Decisions based on weather forecasts were the hardest because people could judge me after the event—better that, though, than being stuck in the mud for a week. Our policy was to keep everyone aware of the issues, but the final decision was always mine.

One time a loud cheer erupted in the bus when, after some deliberation, I said, 'We'll give it a go,' and turned onto the road that everyone except me looked forward to travelling. An angry storm cloud hung off to the south, following our progress all morning with regular rainbows colouring the distant desert scenery. Through the afternoon several more clouds formed, and I felt sick with the decision I'd made that put us all in this situation. First a few drops fell, and I resisted using the wipers because the dust still wasn't settled. By late afternoon we got to the campsite near Mongrel Downs and the heavens opened. Thirty-eight passengers along with the crew of six huddled beneath the dining marquee holding it up with brooms to stop water puddling and hanging onto chairs to stop them blowing away in the tempest of wind, thunder, lightning and pelting rain. Within five minutes it was gone. The sky cleared, and a sensational sunset filled the sky. Overnight, a gentle breeze dried the surface enough to allow an easy camp pack-up and, to our surprise, the road was dry. The storm must have been very localised. We laughed that perhaps our luck was divine intervention because Jack Priest was a passenger on the Bishop's bus. Jack humorously reminded us of his trip to the Canadian

Arctic along with the Lords, Moses and Bishops.

We only needed to make the 2,100 kilometres detour of the Tanami because of rain on four occasions.

Another time we were bound for Tibooburra, Cameron Corner, Innamincka and Birdsville, and the night before leaving the black top, we settled into the White Cliffs Dug Out Hotel on the opal fields of Far West New South Wales. This unique accommodation, like most residences in town, had been dug into the hills to give relief to occupants from sweltering summer temperatures. During the night, we had no clue that a storm raged outside until water starting dripping into the underground rooms, and the lights flickered before going out. We were lucky, because had that rain fallen when we were off the bitumen, we would have been stranded for a couple of weeks by impassable roads.

The worst challenge we ever faced happened in 2010 when deadheading our equipment to Alice Springs for an early start to the winter season. I drove the coach ahead of Lindy, who drove the ute towing a caravan, and behind followed Bruno and Ray in the support truck. About an hour after stopping for breakfast in Balranald, a distraught radio call came from Bruno saying there'd been an accident. With terror in my heart, I turned around. Wreckage lay strewn all over the highway. The ute and caravan had tipped over, and in the distance was a jack-knifed B-Double truck. Bruno, like a real hero, jumped onto the overturned ute with its engine still running and, despite smoke and sparks everywhere, hoisted Lindy out from where she'd been trapped. She was okay but had a broken leg.

Later that day I asked Bruno and Ray to continue up to Alice Springs 1,800 kilometres away, and start preparations for the tour scheduled for departure in just three days. With Lindy in hospital that night, I lay awake thinking of how I could possibly do the season without her. My mind was numb with worry, and if our eldest son, Tom, hadn't taken matters into his own hands, I may have cancelled the whole season. Next day I was inundated with phone calls with willing offers of help, but Tom was already at the airport, from where he rang and said, 'Dad, I'll be in Mildura in a few hours, so just hang on till I get there.' Tom flew his mum back home and took care of her.

Knowing Lindy was in very good hands, and with her encouragement to continue, I set off on the long, lonely drive to Alice Springs. I even turned around before leaving Mildura because I just couldn't face what lay ahead without her. The only thing keeping me going was that I couldn't disappoint the forty excited people expecting to start their tour in just two days. As if I wasn't under enough stress, about half an hour later, I looked behind through glassy eyes to see the trailer swaying around on the safety chains. How much more could I deal with? And when was this nightmare going to end? I launched out of the cab to fix the problem and attacked the rebellious machine like a possessed madman warning that, 'I am in control here—not you, you big heap of German crap.' Within an hour I'd rectified the problem, was back underway and felt much better. It was as if the footy coach had yelled at me at half-time and miraculously snapped me out of my terrible state of mind.

I found it difficult working without Lindy because she always did her job and I did mine, and I had no idea about how she did things. Bruno and I went right back to scratch and agreed there wasn't going to be a right or wrong way for the crew to do things—it was going to be our way. It reminded me of *The Twelfth Man*—a series of Australian comedy productions—when Billy Birmingham famously imitated Ritchie Benaud, saying, 'We work as a team, and we do it my way.'

After completing the first two Kimberly tours, we had just

seven days to deadhead the vehicles to Cairns from Alice Springs and prepare for a Cape York departure. A good mate, Ian Salway, flew out and drove the bus to Cairns for me while I dashed home for a few days.

My time with Lindy was all too short, and when flying back to Cairns from Sydney, the captain made an announcement feared by all airline passengers: 'We have a problem on the flight deck.'

I'd already noticed the sun on the opposite side of the plane, so I knew our course had changed, and the captain confirmed this by telling us we were returning to Sydney. From my window seat, I could see we were flying much lower and slower than normal. When over the Hunter Valley, the wing flaps partially extended, and our speed drastically reduced. The captain said they were burning off fuel to lower the landing weight. We approached Sydney from the east and touched down safely.

Qantas was brilliant, as usual, and I caught a later flight to Cairns, arriving well after dark. Though in one piece, I wondered what was going to happen next.

Bruno and I completed the season as well as we could've hoped for without Lindy, but I remember asking my accountant a year later why she still got half the profits when I did all the work.

~

Sure, we had constant problems and challenges, but we covered enormous distances in the most difficult conditions. Also, we split much of our time between Australia and North America with scheduling so tight that we just couldn't afford machinery breakdowns.

Normally we replaced the support truck every second year

at 60,000 kilometres—because the crews were so hard on it—and replaced the bus after six years at about 400,000 kilometres. This gave us fairly trouble-free operation, but the policy failed drastically one year when a brand-new Nissan Patrol support truck stopped abruptly near Yass when enroute to Alice Springs. We had it towed to Canberra for repair, but the mechanics couldn't find the fault. They replaced various components one by one, and on each occasion, we had to wait a week or so for parts to come from Japan. While waiting through this process, I borrowed my son Tom's work truck. After five weeks without any success and being shifted to a second dealer, the engine of the 'missan Nissan' eventually started. Nobody knew what caused the fault and couldn't say if it might happen again.

Even though we'd owned five Nissans in quick succession, the Nissan company was uninterested in our plight. So I got a permanent-ink marker and turned the sign on the Nissan truck door from Common Rail Turbo Diesel to Common Rubbish Turbo Diesel. The truck was the most photographed and talked about vehicle that year, especially by Toyota owners. When back home and with just 15,000 kilometres on the clock, we sold it, and I've never bought another one.

The 'Missan Nissan'.

The last trip to Cape York with bus number three ran like clockwork for the first nine days, but on the tenth day, the computer fault light flashed, and the engine power cut back to fifty per cent. Luckily, we'd reached the top of Cape York and had several free days scheduled at Bishops Terrace on Loyalty Beach. I spent the whole next day on the phone with a technician in Sydney, trying to find a way to trick the computer to power up for the trip back. Everything we tried failed, so I chartered a Dash 8 aircraft to fly up to Bamaga and return the group to Cairns by the scheduled time. I loaded the crippled bus onto the weekly Jardine Shipping vessel and brought it back to Cairns by sea.

Our group was clearly delighted with the way their tour finished, but we were not. The minor bus electronics problem cost us $38,000.

8

Go Forth a Conqueror.
The Fourth New Bus

(2011)

Though hardly of the same scale as the epic battles in Virgil's writings, in 2011 a great victory for us would've simply been to break even.

In May 2011, I flew alone to Vancouver and took delivery of our fourth new bus and drove it to Whitehorse. The Ford E450 had a twenty-four-seat Starcraft body and had been built specifically for its intended use along the Dempster Highway. From the outside, it looked quite utilitarian, but inside was very plush. The three number plates on the back took me a full year of work to gain—one each for British Columbia, Yukon Territory and Alaska.

Margaret's help was crucial in getting the Yukon plate. She arranged for the government to grant the business licence needed before a commercial bus plate could be issued. Then we used reciprocal rights with British Columbia to get that plate. The

Alaskan plate, however, proved a much more complex process, because it required full motor-carrier compliance in the USA and the issue of a Department of Transportation number linking to the Internal Revenue Service. As part of this process, some months earlier, I'd flown up to Anchorage, Alaska, to meet with a USDOT (United States Department of Transportation) official responsible for ensuring our future compliance. It intrigued him to see a copy of our Australian Compliance package as it was way more stringent than either the USA or Canada. For example, neither country required any vehicle-monitoring or speed-limiting devices, and drivers bought their logbooks at stationary stores. Anyway, I left Anchorage with, as they say up there, 'dool' (dual) international registration.

On the day I took delivery of the fourth new bus, I arrived in Vancouver feeling a bit weary after an overnight flight from Sydney. I started my solo drive to Whitehorse some 2,600 kilometres to the north unconcerned about driving long hours because I wasn't being monitored by a Tachograph or the even-more-feared monitoring device—Lindy. A 6.8 litre V10 petrol engine propelled the little machine with so much power it was hard to keep speed under the limit—and I loved it. In Dawson Creek (not to be confused with Dawson City), I bought all the tools and equipment I needed to carry on the bus.

Travelling the Alcan or Alaska Highway again was just as big a thrill as five years before in the little black Ponti. But this time, being earlier in the year, quite a lot more snow lay on the ground. The further north I travelled, the more difficult radio reception became, until just one station came through. I listened with interest to an interview with TV preacher Harold Camping as he told of his prediction that the world would end on 21 May 2011 and only three per cent of the population would survive.

The spring scenery was simply remarkable. Sunlight

glistened through the icicles hanging from the trees, and porcupines, bears, caribou and sheep were out everywhere in big numbers. In the distance rose the magnificent snow-capped Stone Mountain, and I remember thinking how it would be such a shame if this beautiful place was destroyed in Preacher Camping's impending cataclysm.

Then realisation hit me like a sledgehammer. That day was the 21st of May 2011!

My head was still processing how the day might unfold as the bus started the steep climb up the Stone Mountain. Then all hell broke loose with red warning lights, a piercing alarm and a Stop Immediately message flashing urgently on the dash. I pulled off to the side of the road and, jolted from my disturbed state of mind, quickly shut off the engine. Sitting there in the sudden silence, stranded on the side of a lonely road right out in the middle of nowhere, I said, 'Darn it.' (Official lie.)

A brief inspection revealed a puddle of green engine coolant under the bus. It wasn't the end of the world after all, just a loose hose clamp on a heater hose. Right alongside the bus ran a stream of crystal-clear snow melt water with which to top up the cooling system, and so I resumed the drive. I found it so enjoyable that I slowed down to make it last a little longer.

At Whitehorse I spent several days establishing contacts for bus maintenance and searching for a depot space. Our domicile base in North America became c/- Yukon Alaska Tourist Tours, 91091 Alaska Highway, Whitehorse, YT, Y1A5V9, Canada, behind the Pioneer RV Park. The owner was Morris Kostiuk, a seventy-five-year-old long time Yukoner, and we hit it off right from our first meeting. What I really liked about him was his practical, no-nonsense attitude, enabling him to operate a tough business in a tough environment. His office was typical of many small transport operators with V belts hooked over the backrest of an office chair and a water-pump kit sitting on his desk as a paperweight. The office air was thick with cigarette smoke to the point of being suffocating, and we shared a couple of cheap bourbons from chipped crockery teacups.

After he died in January 2022, I learned of his extraordinary survival following a 1983 plane crash on a remote mountain top in Northern British Columbia. After spending a night on the mountain, suffering from hypothermia and broken legs with no rescue in sight, he took matters into his own hands and started crawling down the mountainside. Although dramatic, this experience is a testament to his strength and determination, but he never mentioned it to me.

At the back of the Pioneer RV Park stood a large shed with features making it a comfortable place to work through the long, dark and cold winters of the Yukon. It had a network of hot-water tubes set into the concrete floor slab, the walls and ceiling were heavily insulated, and a large wood heater stood in the corner. The shed was big enough to park four coaches and still have space for equipment storage and workshop benches. The depot had all the other facilities we needed as well, like a qualified mechanic on site, fuel bowser and wash bay with a water blaster that blew hot water.

Morris, a coach operator himself, had the experience to guide me through the initial set-up phase and subsequent dealings with the Canadian and US transportation authorities. I don't think we would've succeeded with our North American venture without his support. His RV park along the Alaska Highway frontage of his property had massive drive-through sites with power, water, TV and data hook-ups for the giant motorhomes and fifth-wheeler caravans passing through town. Some of those with Florida licence plates provided permanent homes for retirees or itinerant workers following the summer season. Morris' wife,

Greta, was a dynamo in the office and ran a convenience store with unique stocks of local arts, crafts and souvenirs. In the years that followed, we always took our tour groups into Pioneer RV to see our base, and while they browsed Greta's shop, I washed and refuelled the bus and collected the mail.

Bus number four on the Midnight Dome, Yukon Territory, Canada.

We ordered the little bus with several features the Americans at Starcraft had never seen before. Road-camera technology gave passengers a driver's view of the road ahead through multiple TV screens inside the bus. The coach builder took instructions from us on how to set it up and thought the idea was brilliant.

We had this technology on our Australian buses, and passengers loved it. The addition of an onboard fridge and hot water urn facilitated convenient roadside morning-tea and picnic-lunch stops. Behind the bus we towed a small trailer for all the equipment, spares, luggage and catering supplies.

With our own bus in Northern America set up and equipped exactly as we wanted, itineraries to suit our own timing were possible, rather than planning around the availability of 828. In its first year, the new bus made four very happy and uneventful tours to the Canadian Arctic, all departing from Vancouver. All tours now included driving the Alaska Highway for 1,400 kilometres from Dawson Creek to Whitehorse and cruising down the Inside Passage on the AMHS. Eight days longer than previously, this itinerary gave Australians more justification for the long flights over to Canada and back.

The owners of the Days Inn Hotel established a firm relationship with us, and the inn became our Vancouver base for the next five years. Being perfectly placed near the airport, close to the rail system, it gave us easy access into the city and workshops and supply businesses surrounded it. The hotel owners, keen to work with us, concreted a bus parking/wash bay behind the hotel and changed the breakfast buffet to suit the Australian guests—but we had to supply the vegemite. This caused amusement with Canadian Customs whenever we brought large quantities into the country. The nearby River Rock Casino became the venue for meet-and-greet dinners to start each tour.

Now driving rather than flying from Vancouver to Whitehorse, the chances of encountering wildlife became inevitable. Spotting bears brought the most excitement but could be quite dangerous if not handled responsibly. Lindy kept a supply of bear safety leaflets in the bus and made sure our

Australian passengers understood the dangers, and we took bear spray whenever doing short sightseeing walks into the bush. Passengers could expect good, but not numerous, sightings and mostly from the security of the bus or at a safe distance. An exception occurred on the first tour into Stewart BC/Hyder AK in 2011 when we drove past dozens of bears foraging right beside the access road into town. I slowed the bus to walking pace and allowed photographers to sit on the steps and shoot cameras through the open door at such close range that we could smell their breaths. That night in Stewart, the hotel manager gave us all stern instructions about not going outside the hotel for any reason because the town was full of marauding bears rummaging through bins and cars for foodstuffs.

Visiting Stewart was always special because of its location at the tip of the Portland canal, a deep fjord separating Alaska from British Columbia and connecting with the Inside Passage shipping route two hundred kilometres to the south. The two tiny towns of Stewart, British Columbia, and Hyder, Alaska, are only a few kilometres apart, and the road between them follows the shoreline. Usually, thousands of felled pine logs held in huge floating lumber rafts ready to be towed away for milling are tethered just offshore. On a sunny day, the water in the fjord is aqua blue because of the glacial rock flour, but a murky grey if overcast. Awesome views over the Salmon Glacier—the largest glacier in the world with road access—was the highlight of the drive from Hyder up into the mountains along a steep, narrow gravel road. The return drive affords views of the wide glacial outwash plain, where we often saw bald eagles swooping for fish in the shallow braided streams.

The movie *Insomnia* starring Robin Williams, Al Pucino and Hilary Swank, filmed here in 2003, sparked our interest in this area. The scenery was so impressive that we scanned the movie credits hoping to identify the filming location, then we added it to our bucket list of places we just had to visit one day.

Almost as spectacular as the bear sightings on that first tour into Stewart was our witnessing of one of nature's most epic events, the great caribou herds north of the Arctic Circle migrating towards their summer grazing areas. Even though the herd was several kilometres distant, we got a brilliant view from our elevated viewpoint on the Dempster.

Whenever travelling the Alcan, we often saw wild herds of bison grazing along the edges of the highway. These primitive creatures seemed unconcerned about traffic but could react violently if confronted by anyone on foot, especially if the herd contained calves. Stan at Eagle Plain asked me once if I knew the difference between a bison and a buffalo. I didn't, so he told me, 'A buffalo is a big hairy four-legged, horned creature, whereas a bison is what an Australian washes his hands in.'

Mountain goats were common around Stone Mountain as the salt spread by winter road-maintenance crews attracted them to the roadside. Moose were perhaps the hardest animals to see in the wild, and we came to understand why the First Nations people referred to them as the 'shadow dwellers'. Occasionally, though, one would just come out of the bush and run straight across the road in front of us with no traffic sense at all. Even though we seldom saw them, we were always cautious because they could be dangerous. Their main form of defence is to trample with their long gangly legs. I seldom issued a warning about moose attack except at Liard Hot Springs along the Alcan. This swampy location is a natural attraction for the moose because the heat from the springs keeps the surrounding area quite temperate, allowing year-round growth of water grasses. When the military constructed the Alcan during WWII, soldiers developed the area with concrete pools and boardwalks. Moose and bears have killed people there on several occasions.

The little bus travelled 35,000 kilometres in its first year with the only real issue a smashed back window from a stone ricocheting off the luggage trailer. Those of us sitting up the front thought it was quite funny, but the passengers down the back had to wear jackets and sit in the dust until we reached Fort MacPherson, where we made temporary repairs with cardboard and duct tape.

The last trip in 2011 showed us how predictable—to within a few days each year—the onset of the winter freeze-up is up in the Arctic. The road-closure dates are very specific, something that intrigued us. Imagine trying to specify a wet-season road-closure date in tropical Australia!

With the road-closure date of the Dempster in mind, we scheduled the last Arctic tour of the year to only go up as far as the Arctic Circle then turn around and come back for a couple of nights at Eagle Plain on the way back south. Just eighteen days prior, we drove the Dempster in warm weather with the animals still out foraging and the vivid autumn colours still displayed on the lichens and stunted trees alongside the creek banks. In just two-and-a-half weeks, the winter set in. The leaves had all dropped, leaving bare vegetation. Snow covered the mountain ranges, low fog settled into the valleys and the outside temperatures dropped below freezing. When a flurry of snow began falling while heading up the Dempster, I became more cautious and was relieved to reach the Engineers Creek campground for a lunch break. Everyone huddled inside the log cookhouse building and stoked the fire burning in the central wood heater while Lindy served a warming lunch of hot soup with thick slices of buttered bread.

The Dempster carries very little traffic, but no vehicles passed during the hour we were stopped. My anxiety rose because the seven-mile climb up onto the Eagle Plateau, where the weather would be worse, was just up ahead, and the 'rescued tour' had been stranded along this section of the Dempster back in 2006. I made a satellite phone call to Stan at Eagle Plain for some advice.

'Bruce,' he said, 'even the ice road truckers are pulled over up here.'

On that advice we turned around and headed back to Dawson City. I've never been so relieved to get off the Dempster as I was on that day.

Early autumn freeze-up on the Dempster, Yukon Territory, Canada.

~

We learned how to cross international borders and work with transport officials at port-of-entry checking stations. Being an

Australian driver was initially a drawback but eventually became an advantage as border officers became familiar with us. As always, Lindy played a key role with her big smile and by being very organised with the paperwork. She faxed the border station twenty-four hours ahead with a full passenger list and passport numbers so most of the scrutiny had already been done. When we arrived, we handed over all passports stacked in alphabetical order with the green visa-waiver cards completed and enclosed. She accumulated enough of these blank green cards by ransacking every airport we ever transited.

Mostly, people welcomed us as foreign operators, but sometimes we met opposition from Canadians who didn't understand why we were working there. A Ford dealership in Vancouver decided not to service our bus, even though we'd booked it in and left it with them for the whole day. The service manager bluntly asked me if he would be allowed to start up a bus business in Australia. I told him that with his attitude he wouldn't be capable of starting any business. After explaining that we were there at the invitation of his government, he serviced the bus, and I watched closely.

Sometimes, just like in Australia, we encountered issues with small parochial tour operators questioning why travellers would come with us when we weren't Canadian and didn't have a Canadian guide. We had used Canadian guides, but mostly they had no idea about what interested Australians. For example, Canadians wouldn't notice creatures like squirrels and prairie dogs, but they fascinate Australians. Much about North America is similar to Australia, but the few differences are substantial, and if the guides don't recognise what the differences are, they can lose their relevance.

That first year was a steep learning curve, and we were very happy with the end results. Our passengers seemed delighted with their Arctic experiences, authorities hadn't raised any issues about our compliance and not chartering 828 almost offset the cost of the new bus, so we saw the opportunity to crank things up for future years. Both of us enjoyed the season immensely and operating our own little bus added greatly to passenger satisfaction, so I contacted Glen Mason at First Bus Centre in Edmonton about buying a bigger bus.

We did indeed, as Virgil wrote, 'Go forth a conqueror and win great victories' in 2011 because we met our target and broke even. We also fought and won two other mammoth battles, the first being to overcome all our doubts in dealing with border and transport officials, and the second was to defeat the stupidity of the Ford dealership in Vancouver.

9
Henry, the Fifth New Bus

(2012 – 2015)
'Once more unto the breach, dear friends, once more;'
William Shakespeare, King Henry the Fifth

In July 2012 we flew into Edmonton, Alberta, to pick up new bus number five, which we called Henry. On both sides at the front, I stuck a small Super Roo sticker, just like on the side of the famous Australian-built Falcon GT, and like the Falcon, Henry was powerful and a joy to drive. Though built tough for the Dempster, it was also comfortable enough for much longer tours down into the US.

The new machine was a Ford F-650 with a B 6.7 litre Cummins diesel engine, Allison World Series auto and rear air suspension. The body, a thirty-five seat Starcraft, had road-camera technology and a huge walk-in boot at the rear, so we no longer needed to tow a trailer.

Several Canadian Arctic tours and a tour down into the Lower 48—the forty-eight contiguous US States—fully booked Henry's first season. Our licence plates allowed us to take tour groups into the States, but each tour had to start and finish in British Columbia, and no passengers could join when stateside. For the first US tour, we took the safe option of following the same itinerary we'd done several years before with a coach chartered from Vancouver—highlights being Banff, Calgary, Glacier National Park, Great Falls, Mt Rushmore, Devil's Tower, Custer's Battlefield, Yellowstone National Park and Cascades. Everywhere we toured, people commented on what a beautiful bus Henry was, but even though I learned to love it, I thought it was the ugliest thing I ever saw. Its contoured side panels made it difficult to broom wash; the rear overhang was ridiculous, and I bumped my head on the bodywork nearly every time I got out the driver's door.

In the following four years, Henry carried many tour groups down into the Lower 48 to places like Mt St Helens, Yosemite, Death Valley, Las Vegas, Grand Canyon, Zion National Park, Bryce Canyon, Monument Valley, Mesa Verde in Colorado, Arches National Park, Salt Lake City and Yellowstone National Park.

To meet the demand, we worked both the spring and autumn seasons, and eventually North American tours amounted to half our total turnover. It was a wonderful experience, and often I looked out through the windscreen from the driver's seat with such joy that it all felt like a dream.

"Henry" in Arches National Park, Utah, USA.

Mostly, things ran very smoothly because road conditions were so much better than in Australia even along the Dempster, causing few of the machinery problems we had back home. However, issues still arose without warning that sometimes had nothing to do with the bus.

One incident stretched my ability to cope in the face of possible disaster. I sat in the bus parked outside the terminal building at Inuvik airport, NWT, Canada, waiting for a tour group to fly back after a day at Tuktoyaktuk. The flight was late, but low clouds often caused delays. After another hour or so of waiting, panic gripped me when fire engines, police cars, ambulances and rescue vehicles raced into the airport with lights flashing. I spoke to the RCMP officer in charge of the emergency services and asked him what was going on, but he couldn't tell me due to RCMP policy. I let him know I was the tour leader of a group overdue from Tuk, and then he confirmed that it was indeed a flight from Tuk in considerable trouble.

Feeling numb with fear, I went outside to get a better view of the runway and saw the twin-engine aircraft do several low circuits past the control tower. The landing gear was down but not the nose wheel. The next ten minutes were extremely tense as I watched the emergency vehicles take positions along the runway.

I'd watched this type of situation many times before on TV, but believe me, when it happens in real life, it's terrifying. The stricken aircraft made its cautious approach and landed with nose held up until there was no more lift coming from the wings. Then the nose dropped to the ground and both propellers belted the tarmac skewing the plane off the runway onto the grass. Emergency vehicles quickly surrounded the aircraft, and the terrified passengers evacuated. The group returned safely to Earth thanks to the pilot's extraordinary skill. When they got back to the terminal I was there to hug and console them, but it occurred to me later that perhaps they were consoling me.

Some months later, I learned that that aircraft would never fly again due to the damage.

Many of the other problems we encountered were just minor annoyances, like people leaving medications behind in hotel fridges and losing passports and so on.

Most Australian passengers found travelling in North America a real thrill, and we listened with great interest to what highlights they loved the best. On Arctic tours the universal opinion was that staying at Eagle Plain Hotel and cruising down the Inside Passage aboard the MV Matanuska topped the list.

'Eagle' perches high on a range just thirty kilometres to the south of the Arctic Circle at the halfway point along the

Dempster. Built in the late 1970s, although quite basic, it has a warm homely feel. The hotel and roadhouse staff always treated us like family, and our passengers enjoyed mingling with adventurous travellers, road-maintenance workers and ice road truckers. Perhaps an even bigger attraction, though, was the real possibility of seeing the northern lights. Evelyn, the German bar manager, was a night owl and always kept an eye on the night skies, especially when it became darker later in the season. If she thought we might see the aurora borealis (or northern lights), she made a list of all those wishing to be woken. If the call came, excited people stampeded down the corridor and out the back door. On those clear, icy nights, the spectacle was often so good that we heard the 'arcing' sound often associated with the lights. A wooden viewing deck elevated sightseers high enough to get an unobstructed view to the horizon all around.

Luckily, most folk outside the hotel on those special nights were unaware of the danger of bears drawn to the hotel by the aromas wafting from the kitchen. Inconspicuously, Eleanor or Evelyn armed themselves with a rifle loaded with rubber bullets and stood ready to shoot if necessary. One night some bears got right into the hotel and tore the shop apart, placing house guests and staff in great danger.

Over time we got to know some of the regular road workers and truckers who stayed there quite well. Lindy even arranged an eightieth birthday cake for her favourite grader driver. Apparently, it was the first time in his life he'd ever had a birthday cake of his own. He was one of the people we met when we first drove up in the Ponti, and he'd helped rescue Bruno and Christine's group years before.

The MV Matanuska was the other best-loved highlight according to most of our passengers and became known among them as 'Eagle Plain afloat'. Like Eagle, it was old but very homely, and groups relaxed as soon as they boarded in Skagway, Alaska (AK), probably because they'd travelled five thousand kilometres in the bus by this time. It was part of the Alaska Marine Highway System connecting the Alaskan coastal communities to the outside world. On board was a lounge bar where the staff encouraged passengers to entertain at night if they played an instrument or could sing, recite poetry or crack a few jokes. On one very special trip we had a bush poet, Greg Scott, who headlined shows at Tamworth each year, plus singers Peter Fahey, Glenda Bain and Carol Wood, who also accompanied on guitar. We had such a great night that the ship's crew talked about it for years afterwards. During the daytime, passengers could sit in the forward viewing lounge and listen to either a parks or forestry officer giving commentary about the wildlife, glaciers and history along the spectacular Inside Passage route. Matanuska was just within the limits to fit through the Wrangel Narrows where the navigation channel gave just a metre of clearance under the keel at low tide, and the banks either side were very close. It was so tight that a crewmember stood up on the bow waving flags to assist the captain to navigate between the buoys along the zig zag channel.

We disembarked at Prince Rupert, BC, three days later. Our timing depended on tides and scheduling, but mostly we arrived very early in the morning. Getting through the Canadian border station was the first obstacle, because one of the officials was hung up about foreigners like us operating in her country, and she always gave us trouble. It started the first time we drove off the 'Mat' and into the station at three in the morning when we were all still half asleep. She took our paperwork, told us to wait where we were and went inside. We sat for two hours in the cold before I followed her inside only to get a gob full of abuse on how she'd told me to stay in the bus. She couldn't find anything obviously wrong with the paperwork; it just didn't seem right to her that an Australian could do what we were doing in 'her' country. This happened several times before I communicated with the Canadian Consul General in Sydney about the issue. After that it never happened again.

Most border crossings went very smoothly because we prepared everyone on procedures, but for some obscure reason, many Australians tried to imitate Crocodile Dundee in these situations by exaggerating pronunciations and trying to be funny. Once we all had a good laugh when crossing into the USA with a passenger celebrating his eightieth birthday. The border official said, 'Well, pops, we won't be needing fingerprints from you anymore because you're no longer considered a threat to the United States.' The whole place erupted in laughter, including the officials.

The next obstacle was the Transport Port of Entry Checking Station. On one occasion an inspector looked at my logbook and commented on its neatness, so I thanked him for the compliment. Morris later told me that they check the neat ones most thoroughly because those drivers are mostly more educated and more likely to diddle the system. Some of the transport officers even wore side arms, like in cowboy movies, so I was always very polite.

Apart from Eagle and the Mat, a few days spent enjoying the attractions in our domicile town of Whitehorse brought great enjoyment. The Frantic Follies Show, Yukon Transportation Museum, Yukon Fish Ladder, Log Cabin Skyscraper, Beringia Centre, Miles Canyon Suspension Bridge, SS Klondike sternwheeler, MacBride Museum, waterfront tram, float-plane fishing trips, husky dog farm, Yukon Wildlife Preserve, the Klondike Rib and Salmon Bake, MV Schwatka and the giant, ninety-nine cent cinnamon rolls at Tim Hortons. There was just so much to do there, and we felt proud to present our Canadian hometown as best we could to all who travelled with us.

One day while a group enjoyed a ride along the banks of the Yukon River on the Waterfront Tram, they saw several suited men standing outside the court building in the cold. The tram driver loudly announced over the PA, 'Gee, it must be cold today because those lawyers have their hands in their own pockets.'

Another time on the first cruise of the season aboard the MV Schwatka through the Yukon River's Miles Canyon, I was in the wheelhouse with the captain when, despite setting both engines at full throttle, we barely made any headway against the immense river flow. For thirty minutes the engine sat dangerously on the red line at maximum revs but we had no option to turn around in the confined cliff-lined canyon. We made it through, but the captain confessed later that it was a very close call.

~

Maintaining a bus in North America when constantly on the move required effort at most stops during the day or at hotels in the evenings. Often little 'niggles' with the machine kept me busy, like on one southbound trip along I-5 through Washington, Oregon and northern California in the rain when a fuse kept blowing, causing the main computer to cut the engine power back to fifty per cent. Eventually, after several days of searching, I found a tiny water drip under the dash that caused the problem.

In Las Vegas I needed to clean the air conditioner return air filter, so I removed it and took it up to the hotel room to wash it in the bathtub. Being short of time, I didn't clean the tub nor tell Lindy, so when seeing it, she assumed a serious plumbing problem and called hotel maintenance. A ring of dirty lint clung to the tub around the waterline, and the staff were shocked and baffled at what might be the cause. They couldn't convince Lindy, who thought they weren't being truthful, and she gave them a hard time.

On another occasion when pulling out of a parking area, I caught the edge of the rear bumper on a post and bent it badly. I fixed it by backing square on to the same post until it was straight again.

Our Australian accent caused some issues because people listened to how we said things rather than what we said. Americans can understand when they try, but some words have very different meanings in either country. A good example of this happened to us at a bar in Great Falls, Montana, when, along with several other Australians, we ordered a round of drinks from the waitress. Being hot, I harmlessly asked for a couple of jugs of beer, please. She gasped, took a step backwards and looked disgusted with me. The Australians looked at each other in disbelief at her reaction to what was, to us, a totally normal request.

Feeling uncomfortable, I gestured pouring from a jug, to which she said with some relief, 'Oh, you want a pitcher.'

Stupidly, I thought she said 'picture' and replied, 'No, I want the real thing.' (In America 'jugs' are female breasts.)

Even more amusing to us, a waitress in a hamburger joint in Decatur, Alabama, got the giggles when talking with us because of the funny way we spoke. Imagine that—an Alabamian laughing at the way we speak.

My favourite American was Samantha Garmin, who knew more about the country than anyone else. I never met her personally, but her patient voice guided me through every town, city and along country roads for many years. If ever I missed a turn, even though given plenty of notice, she politely asked me to make a U-turn using the word 'please' freely and never getting frustrated with me. How different to Lindy Garmin in Australia, who had less equanimity, telling me where I should have turned after driving past it.

On another US tour, an issue arose that had nothing to do with language confusion. At Zion National Park in Utah, the entry-gate guard directed me to the bus parking area, where all the passengers got off and headed into the park. Shortly afterwards, a young park ranger abruptly and rudely ordered me to move the bus to the proper parking area. Politely, I answered that the gate guard told me to park here. In a temper, the ranger threatened to call security. I enjoyed telling him that he was the first American I'd ever met that I didn't like. Then I pointed at another bus unloading passengers beside me and told him to leave me alone and go and annoy them. And he did.

That same day I briefed our group about the need to be back at the bus before 4:00 pm because we had a pilot vehicle booked to escort us through a narrow tunnel up in the mountains above us. All tunnel traffic would be stopped at exactly 4:45 pm to let us through, and if we were late, we would be trapped on the wrong side of the mountain for the night. By 4:15 pm two ladies hadn't returned, so when 4:25 pm came, I unloaded their luggage along with Lindy's and shut the bus door. Lindy planned to wait for them and somehow catch up with us next day. As we set off, someone spotted them running towards us. We arrived at the tunnel just as the pilot vehicle started through. The ladies were so embarrassed that one of them, Elle from Perth in Tasmania, made a fresh batch of scones for every tour group we ever took through her town—enough for the whole busload.

~

Christine found an excellent wholesale booking agent based

in Chicago, who booked all hotels and attractions for us and sent a single invoice. She was expert at winning ballots for the high-demand accommodations in Yosemite and Grand Canyon National Parks, so we very seldom missed out. All arrangements were faultless except once when, through a misunderstanding (my fault), the bookings were confirmed for one day later than intended.

We crossed into the US from Canada without knowing about the error and arrived at the hotel near Mt St Helens a day earlier than the booked date. The hotel manager thought he'd made the mistake and gave us the best stay we'd ever had there. But when we arrived in McMinnville, Oregon, on the second night, still not realising the error, we found the hotel staff there blunt and unhelpful. Fortunately, the agent in Chicago quickly booked us into another hotel for the night. Correcting the error at that late stage was impractical, especially because we'd won the ballots at Yosemite and Grand Canyon for the days ahead.

We consulted with the tour group and, luckily, most passengers were happy to add an extra day and arrive back in Vancouver a day later than scheduled. Fortunately, we knew the area around McMinnville in the Willamette Valley quite well, so we easily kept everyone occupied for the extra day. Several years beforehand, we'd driven through there doing tour research work, and the fertility of the farmlands had impressed us, so we spent time exploring. European settlement started there in the mid-1800s, when several hundred thousand people with 'Oregon Fever' arrived in wagon trains after braving six months on the famous Oregon Trail hoping for the rewards of free land. These brave, ambitious and robust pioneers thrived where the land was fertile and the climate mild and wet.

When driving among the farms, we spotted the tail section of a 747 jumbo jet jutting up above the trees several miles away, so we drove in that direction to investigate. We discovered a jumbo sitting high up off the ground on the roof of a waterpark, and alongside it was an even bigger surprise—a huge glass-fronted building housing the famous Spruce Goose aircraft built by Howard Hughes during WWII. We thought it lived at Long Beach, California, where we'd seen it in 1982, but no, it was right there in front of us in a huge shed on the outskirts of the little rural town of McMinnville, eighty kilometres south of Portland, Oregon.

The group spent their extra day very happily at the Evergreen Aviation Museum that, along with the Spruce Goose, housed an SR-71 Blackbird (the fastest plane on earth), space capsules from the Gemini and Apollo era and an Imax theatre. We wondered why we hadn't heard much about it before.

We got some justice when we stayed the next night at the intended hotel in McMinnville. Without our knowledge, the group wreaked revenge on the hotel by ransacking the breakfast buffet. They stripped it bare, and at morning-tea stops for days afterwards produced vast quantities of pastries, fruit and muesli bars.

Our Australian groups were a pleasure to host, and we were always very proud to travel with them. Often we heard their stories about how the locals they met were so welcoming and friendly they even anonymously paid their restaurant bills for them. Hotel staff constantly told us that our groups were a pleasure to host because they were so much fun and very considerate.

We were ashamed at one exception, though. It occurred at the evening flag-lowering ceremony at Mt Rushmore, in the Black Hills of South Dakota. A crowd nearing five thousand patriotic Americans sat reverently in the amphitheatre below the enormous, sculptured mountain face of four former US presidents and watched 'Old Glory' being lowered. The master of ceremonies invited all veterans in the crowd onto the stage to loud applause and, at the most moving point, in total silence, two ladies in our group stood up and yelled, 'Aussie, Aussie, Aussie.' We couldn't believe their poor judgement, but, before we reacted, others in our group made it clear to them that this was unacceptable.

Touring in North America was always filled with surprises, like the day we got the fright of our lives when driving down into Death Valley. Without warning, a military jet streaked past us at eye level, perhaps just several hundred metres in front, blasting noise and a shock wave so severe it rocked the bus and felt like being hit over the back of the head with a cricket bat. Then a second aircraft, hot on the tail of the first, belted past hitting us with a second shock wave. Instinctively, I stopped the bus and, when I could, checked for damage and to see if anyone had been traumatised. By this time the dog-fighting aircraft were so high in the sky above that they were almost out of sight, but still the pursuit continued. Edwards Airforce Base and the Mojave Desert weren't far to the south, so perhaps we saw Maverick or Iceman from *Top Gun*.

Over time we established many close contacts in the industry, people who loved working with our groups, like Mike, a guide on the JFK Trolley Tram Tours in Dallas, Texas. We first met him when exploring Dallas for future tours, and we were the only two passengers on one of his trams. He joked that he wasn't expecting much gratuity because Australians are notorious for not tipping, but it didn't matter because they were always so much fun. Mike gave us the best two-hour tour we ever did, so we surprised him with a big tip and by promising him all our future group bookings in Dallas.

Often passengers had extraordinary interest and knowledge

about specific places and subjects, so touring with us allowed them to further their quest for information and, in most cases, visit for the first time. For example, I shared my boyhood interest in the Alaska Highway and Civil War battles of the Deep South with many others, but one of the most interesting passengers with a special subject knowledge was David Kemp, who had a passion for country music. He joined our Lone Star, Dixieland, Music City Tour that allowed him several days in Nashville, Tennessee. We noticed his excitement level building the closer we got to Nashville while travelling through the cotton fields and Civil War sites of Louisiana and Mississippi. Still a day away, he asked if the tour group might like to hear of his lifelong desire to get to Nashville, along with a little of its history. He took over the microphone and CD player on the coach and explained why so much music of all genres comes out of Nashville. The things he told us enriched the time we spent at the Country Music Hall of Fame and the famous Studio B at RCA Records, and our evening at the Grand Ole Opry was the experience of a lifetime. David's other special interest appealed to me more than most, and we spent hours engrossed in discussion about old buses, Bedford trucks and Denning gearshift patterns while Lindy and David's wife, Ruth, yawned with disinterest.

Having personal friends travel with us in North America was always good, but, for obvious reasons, we were always very careful not to treat them differently to everyone else. One exception to this friends' policy occurred by accident when we anticipated having to deadhead the Henry bus 2,600 kilometres to Whitehorse prior to a tour. My good mate 'Clod' Emery, the owner of a large compost/soil company operating several dozen large trucks, offered to fly over to Canada early to help me with the deadhead drive. When we finalised the itinerary, however, we incorporated that section into the tour, but Clod still wanted to help me with the driving. I gave him a list of requirements to legalise his participation when carrying passengers, including things like having a comprehensive USDOT (United States Department of Transportation) medical examination, which he did. Clod seemed very comfortable in the driver's seat but clearly struggled keeping the speed down. He commented on how powerful the machine was, but it didn't occur to me until later that he wouldn't have known how nice it was to drive a Ford because he was a Holden man.

We ran North American tours the same way as in Australia, stopping for roadside morning teas and picnic lunches. Whether it was the culture or the colder climate, suitable parks were hard to find, but over time we got to know where they were and sometimes shared these places with American tour operators, who always commented on what a great idea roadside catering was.

Sometimes in America we noticed deficiencies compared to what we had in Australia, and we were always alert for new business opportunities to exploit this. When waiting at the Boeing factory at Everett, Washington, while our group took a tour, I went to a nearby liquor store to buy a cask of red wine, and the server told me to go to a winery. My head went into a spin at the business possibilities of introducing wine casks to America. I said, with amazement, that back home we have an Australian invention called a wine cask that's a bladder bag contained in a cardboard box.

'Oh, you want a bag in a box,' she said. 'We have pallets of them out the back.'

~

Just like in Australia, we invited passengers to take the microphone and tell their life stories if they wished. On one very memorable trip up the Dempster, Ellis Nicholson mentioned his approaching milestone wedding anniversary. I quizzed him later that night in the lounge at Eagle Plains, and he told me their fortieth wedding anniversary was the next day, the thirty-first of August 2014. Lindy arranged for a special table in the hotel at Inuvik just for Ellis and Bronwyn, plus us. Passengers sitting together beside us wondered what was going on.

During dinner, I rose to propose a toast, saying, 'Folks, forty years ago today, in a little church in Grenfell, New South Wales, Bronwyn and Ellis were married.' We toasted the couple to loud applause. Then, back on my feet, I said with a little falter in my voice, 'But, folks, you won't believe the coincidence because on that very same day, in a little church in Berry, New South Wales, so were Lindy and I.' It was a night we shall never forget.

Wildlife spotting along the Dempster, Northwest Territories, Canada.

~

By the end of our fourth season with the Henry bus, demand for Canadian Arctic tours began to slow down as we exhausted our pool of Australian travellers. We considered boosting things with expensive advertising, but that was a bit too risky for our small operation.

In 2015 we headed up to the Arctic as usual, not knowing it was to be Henry's last tour for us. For several months prior to the last tour, we'd stored the bus in the depot of a large bus company, but when I went to get it, I noticed it in the workshop. I was surprised to hear that it had a faulty starter motor that needed replacing. That seemed a little strange because such a problem was rare with a relatively young vehicle. If the jacket heater hadn't been plugged-in through the winter, an apprentice might have over-cranked the engine, but, whatever the cause, machines have a habit of surprising operators with problems.

They delivered the repaired bus to us at midnight before our departure for Whitehorse next morning, so we woke early and cleaned, loaded and refuelled it ready for departure at eight. Even though hectic that morning, I still loved driving out of Vancouver following the same route we first drove in the little black Ponti ten years earlier. Through the CBD and Stanley Park, over the Lions Gate Bridge and around the magnificent coastline of Howe Sound, one of the many fjords north of Vancouver. Both of us got a real kick listening to passengers commenting on the most basic Canadian differences at our first stop below the Stawamus Chief for morning tea. The 'Chief' is one of the largest granite monoliths in the world, and rock climbers come from all over the world to climb the cliff face. We found watching the thrill seekers interesting but not as much as observing our passengers tuning into many of the simple differences in Canada, like the smell of the air in the pine forest, the sounds made by the birds and seeing the proliferation of huge pickup trucks. It was a spectacular start to each tour.

The tour continued normally for the 2,600 kilometres

to Whitehorse, taking in all the highlights now so routine and familiar to us—a group photo at Mile One of the Alaska Highway, stroll over the curved WWII wooden Kiskatanaw bridge and time to browse the signpost forest at Watson Lake. The 'forest' started with a homesick soldier nailing a mileage sign pointing to his hometown in Illinois during the wartime highway construction, and the idea caught on among other soldiers and continues to this day with travellers from all over the world. The forest now covers several acres, and a sign already pointed to Nowra, New South Wales, Australia, so we didn't need to add one ourselves.

Another Bishops group at Mile One, Dawson Creek, BC, Canada.

In Whitehorse, the Frantic Follies show always gave us a big laugh, so we sat any 'characters' in the front row so they could be embarrassed during the audience participation segments.

Another part of the tour passengers loved was visiting the historic little cabin in Dawson City where the poet Robert Service lived during the great Klondike gold rush and wrote many of his wonderful poems. I became a great admirer of his works after Lindy dragged me along to a recital despite my disinterest, and she has gloated ever since. I parked beside the cabin and ushered the group inside to enjoy a ranger-led inspection and brilliant poetry recital.

Afterwards, I couldn't start the bus because the new starter motor wouldn't engage. Thankfully we weren't stranded up along the remote Dempster with an issue like this. On inspection I found the ring gear completely gouged away but, astonishingly, saw no signs of any metal fragments in the flywheel housing—as if it had been flushed out. I suspected that the starter motor had been 'borrowed' when the bus was in storage at the bus depot in Vancouver and replaced with the wrong one. The Cummins engine now had a Ford starter, not a Cummins, and repairs now required removing the gearbox. It was a long weekend, so I probably couldn't order the parts until the following Tuesday, meaning we could be stranded for a week. Luckily, next day I found a dealership south of Vancouver with the parts in stock and paid a fortune to get them airfreighted to Dawson City, but heavy clouds prevented any flights landing that weekend. I tried to get a replacement vehicle, but nothing was available. Being a long weekend, Morris at Yukon Alaska Tourist Tours had no driver available and 828 was away with another group. Also, the owners of 828 had recently introduced a policy to never allow any of their coaches on the Dempster again following a CAD $250,000 repair to one of their newer model coaches after it was damaged up there.

I didn't sleep for forty-eight hours while under so much stress but finally used my get-out-of-jail-free card given to me

214

several years earlier by an impressive young bloke we met on an Air North flight from Vancouver to Whitehorse. He sat beside us and became inquisitive at the number of people walking past our seats saying g'day with broad Australian accents. When he realised we were escorting a group of thirty, he quizzed us on what enticed us to the Yukon Territory from the opposite side of the world. My answer impressed him and he gave us his business card along with an invitation to contact him directly if we ever needed help with our Yukon endeavours. To our amazement we'd been talking to the son of Joseph Sparling, Air North's co-founder, majority owner and hands-on CEO as head pilot. He started commercial aviation in 1977 with a Cessna and grew the operation to include six Boeing 737s and many smaller aircraft capable of servicing isolated communities with gravel airstrips.

When the people at Air North heard of our plight, they quickly reconfigured and dispatched a medium-sized turbo-prop aircraft (Hawker Siddeley HS 748) to Dawson City, collected our group with luggage and flew us to Inuvik. Next morning, we boarded the short flight over the Mackenzie delta to Tuktoyaktuk, landed on the gravel airstrip and waited several hours while we enjoyed a special guided tour of the Inuit community and finally returned us to Whitehorse where Donna and 828 were waiting to rescue us again. Air North chartered that flight to us in good faith that we would make payment when banks reopened after the long weekend. The team at Air North reflected the typical attitude we often saw among Yukoners and obviously influenced hugely by their hands-on CEO, Joseph Sparling. Up in the Yukon Territory, one person in twelve either works for the airline or owns shares.

When we left Dawson City on that Air North charter flight, I had no idea we would never see Henry again. For several weeks it sat out on the street beside Robert Service's little cabin before being repaired in Dawson City and driven to the depot in Whitehorse by Lorne, one of Morris' drivers. It sat for months while we contemplated the future of our North American tour operations. Regardless, another year at least would take us back because we already held firm bookings from about forty very keen people. Eventually, we accepted it would be irresponsible and reckless to risk passenger security without a reliable contingency plan for bus issues. I contemplated acquiring an old vehicle similar to 828 to leave on standby at Whitehorse, but the experience with 49 taught us that high overhead costs can quickly destroy viability. Morris resolved our dilemma by volunteering his coach for one more trip up the Dempster even though he worried about doing it.

Glen Mason in Edmonton sold Henry for us, and it went to its new life in Yellowknife in the Northwest Territories.

~

2016 was our final year touring in the Arctic and leaving Vancouver in a chartered coach felt like turning the clock back. The driver, a mature-aged fellow named Marvin, accepted the task of driving us 2,150 kilometres to Watson Lake, where we would transfer into one of Morris' coaches for the more adventurous run up along the Dempster.

The first night north of Vancouver at 100 Mile House, Marvin sat out on the patio of the hotel with a slab of beer, drinking until quite late in the evening. He didn't look so good, next day, so I sat right behind him with my seat belt unfastened and closely watched his every move. My plan was to grab the controls from him if he dozed off and, luckily, I did because I had to jolt him when a large grizzly bear ran across the road in front of the coach. How he missed it is still a mystery.

This last tour was memorable because my much-loved cousin Barbara and husband Graham travelled with us, and when the sad news of my father's passing reached us, their presence was especially comforting. We didn't tell the tour group because of our policy that it is not about us, and we owed all our attention to the passengers.

Good friends Patrick and Jeanette Muller from Nowra also travelled with us on that last tour, and unbeknown to us, they heard of my father's passing from family back home. This placed them in an awkward situation as they wondered if we knew.

For about another week, we disguised all the arrangements we were making behind the scenes, then eventually I announced I was flying home early, leaving Lindy behind to lead the last three days of the tour. I'd been asked to deliver the eulogy, so I planned many reflective hours high over the Pacific.

Before boarding the Air North 737 at Whitehorse Airport, I looked with a heavy heart at the place we happily called our second home for ten years. I hesitated at the door of the aircraft to suck in one last deep breath of cool, fresh Yukon air. A verse of poetry by Robert Service rang in my head:

> *There's a land where the mountains are nameless,*
> *And the rivers all run God knows where;*
> *There are lives that are erring and aimless,*
> *And deaths that just hang by a hair;*
> *There are hardships that nobody reckons;*
> *There are valleys unpeopled and still;*
> *There's a land—oh, it beckons and beckons,*
> *And I want to go back—and I will.*

As yet, I haven't been back—but I will.

10
Six and Out!
The Sixth New Bus

(Back to 2012)

I bought the sixth new bus with Lindy's full approval but on the condition that it would be the last.

Number six was another MAN with an automated manual twelve-speed transmission and air suspension front and back. Driving it was like heaven on wheels, and passengers loved it as much as I did, even though I was scared stiff of it. My confidence with technology had been damaged by the Cape York electronics issue with bus three, and this new machine was riddled with it. A computer screen positioned in front of the driver constantly displayed annoying and distracting messages, and if a door wasn't shut properly, the machine objected and threw a tantrum. This level of technology is good if always on bitumen roads and near to civilisation, but just imagine the risks in the outback. Unlike our bigger competitors, we relied completely on just this one bus.

Bus number six after another crossing of the Tanami.

Driving it was astonishing compared to the beasts we used fifteen years before, and it gave us years of trouble-free service. Its computer-controlled gear shifting was better than the most experienced driver could do, and it was so soft and quiet to drive it spoiled getting into the Landcruiser. On rough gravel roads, I was often shocked to see how fast we were travelling and consciously slowed to save punishing the running gear too much.

Number six took us all over Australia from the narrow high-altitude tracks of the Snowy Mountains to beach driving near Esperance, through the Tarkine wilderness in Tasmania and all the major outback gravel highways. When our youngest son, Andy, got married, we polished it up, draped ribbons on the front and carried guests to the reception on top of Berry Mountain.

Around this time the baby boomer generation started travelling with us. The first tough lesson we learned was that our tours were no longer the premium choice for adventure travel, but the budget option to having a fully equipped Landcruiser 200 series towing a Bushtraker, go-anywhere caravan.

This was blatantly obvious the last time we stayed on Bishop's Terrace at Loyalty Beach. I noticed something very different near our camp and interrupted Lindy as she busily prepared dinner. I pointed to all the campsites spread along the waterfront occupied by very expensive caravans, all with raised satellite dishes and owners sitting outside on portable lounge chairs. While the sun set over the Torres Strait, couples wearing trendy casual wear poured sparkling wines into elegant glass flutes. We both thought how good it looked, but the point I was making was that things had changed.

Just twenty-five years before, the average unshaven motorist to Cape York drove a Toyota tray back with tinnie boat on top and lived on beer and fish. To get there they needed a spirit of adventure like that of Burke and Wills and the 4WD experience of the Leyland brothers.

Early in the process of generational change, a passenger claiming to also speak for several others ambushed me, saying they wanted to change the tour route. He was quite emphatic and produced a map showing their proposal. I knew the track he suggested and explained issues like difficult creek crossings, low overhanging branches and considerably longer trip time. But he persisted and suggested it should be put to a vote. Maybe I could have handled this better, but I beckoned him over to the side of the bus and pointed to the Bishop's Adventures sign displayed prominently. I said, 'That's me, and it's not a democracy, mate.'

Luckily, he cracked up laughing and let the idea go.

The baby boomers were fun to travel with, but many things that worked before, no longer worked with them. For example, playing music in the bus caused annoyance rather than pleasure. I missed being able to use it to manage passengers by sending them off to sleep when not much was happening and wake them when needed. Also, tour commentaries had to be faultless because they 'Google' checked everything I said.

One time, while I conversed with a passenger about how different it was now, a lady nearby interrupted and said, 'I'm a baby boomer and I'm not like that.'

No, she wasn't. She was worse. Before the tour, she phoned every motel to arrange her special list of requirements, including things like four medium-softness pillows and a room not cleaned with any chemicals.

Others bombarded us with their special dietary requirements that mostly Lindy was happy to work with, but one request was for no foods grown underground.

How things had changed in just thirty years, not only with passenger expectations but in many other things like communications. When first touring on Cape York we hired an HF radio from the Royal Flying Doctor Service in Cairns so big that it packed into a large canvas bag. The aerial was a long wire needing to be thrown over a tree and only night-time calls were possible due to daytime atmospheric noises. Later we bought a Codan HF system with an auto-tuning aerial and a facility for making radio telephone calls by 'patching' through to the telecom base in Darwin. Our first satellite phone packed into a large case that doubled as the satellite dish, but very long delays made conversations difficult. Finally, satellite phones were just as simple to use as a normal cell phone.

The baby boomers embraced technology, and for us, it was

revolutionary. Lindy paid the business accounts from anywhere in the world; I did trip research on the internet and even selected hotels based on street-view images. Technicians on the other side of the globe could diagnose any vehicle issues, and where once we would've mailed a ute load of letters, now Christine did it all from a computer keyboard. Best of all, I could listen to the football live instead of calling home to find out the score. If my Dragons ever lost, the boys made this a miserable task for me.

~

Sometimes Lindy was brave enough to ponder with me what life after travel might look like, but the truth was that our business would be difficult to sell as a going concern. We shared office, labour and workshop resources with the local Bigfoot operation, and we'd been draining profits away for years to lift Bigfoot to where it would support our retirement.

Late one night I received a phone call from Colin Fitzgerald up in Kununurra, Western Australia, asking what plans we had for the coming years and expressing interest in buying our bus and Bush Lodge equipment. Colin was an enterprising tourism operator in the Kimberley with caravan parks, charter cruises, permanent camps, car hire and bus tours. Incredibly, just before he phoned, Lindy and I had been discussing this very issue and getting a little frustrated with each other. Eventually, after many weeks of negotiation, we did a deal and faced the real possibility that we'd done our last bus trip because, just months before, we'd sold Henry and ceased North American tours.

Lindy was correct by pushing us both in this direction because, at that time, we had elderly parents, adult children and grandchildren at the stage where our help was much needed. We also wanted to reconnect with our own friends, those we hadn't seen much for thirty years, unless they'd joined us on tour.

In a whirlwind we moved into a little beach house overlooking the river at Shoalhaven Heads in the same street as our son Tom and his young family, and just a three-minute drive from the Bigfoot base and new main office.

Bruno and Christine also made the sea-change move to Shoalhaven Heads to be closer to work and where Bruno could enjoy more time fishing. Bruno led a team of four Bigfoot drivers, and Christine shared the ticket office and general office duties with Lindy, leaving each of them plenty of grandmother time. Much of my time was spent either in the workshop or out on the tractor maintaining the same country I had as a boy.

The four of us worked together as happily as we'd always done.

For over thirty years, the Bigfoot business just kept plodding along and steadily growing. From being just a small operation on weekends and school holidays it grew to being an all-year-round attraction for thousands of domestic and international passengers each month. The two machines were mechanically and structurally identical to bus three but with open sides and huge tractor wheels.

Business flourished when daily busloads of international visitors started coming through, and that took eight years of effort and expense to establish. Our second son Joe was the instigator and driving force in the early years of this process. Working with large bus groups of international visitors was quite easy for us because we understood their operational issues better than most due to our own bus experiences in North America and Australia.

The name Bigfoot amused many Chinese passengers because

that term to them means a bossy woman—the type that didn't follow the old foot-binding ritual.

Our modest attraction formed an important link in a chain of businesses including Dolphin Watch Cruises on Jervis Bay, several other local attractions, plus agents, hotels, carriers, duty free shops and so on. Bigfoot appeared on TV screens and travel brochures all over the world and was a key attraction, especially on the rare occasions when weather prevented cruising on the bay. International travellers allowed us to maintain daily departures even through the domestic low season. The unexpected benefit was an increase in business because a crowd attracts a crowd. In 2019 we carried 20,000 plus passengers to the mountain summit on the two big machines.

Bigfoot machines, 2019.

~

Not long after selling bus number six, I became very restless about not having a bus, and when I stumbled upon a couple of nice little Mercedes coaches for sale, I bought them to give us something to work with while contemplating how and when to exit from bus touring. We took them to Tasmania, Flinders Ranges, Eyre Peninsula, Great Ocean Road, Victorian High Country, Yerranderie, Gippsland, O'Reilly's and on many short local tours. We underutilised them, but it was good to have a spare bus if needed.

On a Great Ocean Road tour, one of the little coaches started playing up, so I called my mate Ian Salway, one of our Bigfoot drivers, and asked him to get the spare bus down to Colac 970 kilometres south as soon as he could. He arrived very late that night, and next morning the passengers noticed two very similar machines parked out the back of the motel. At breakfast we listened with amusement to all the chatter, and all I told them was that the bus had a mechanical issue, and a substantial prize would be awarded to anyone identifying the problem. This was my little game after thirty years of listening to experts after the event. Apparently, the whatchamacallit was making a funny noise and the whoozeewhatsit was rattling and maybe the thingamabob was interfering with the thingamajig.

~

Generally, folks travelling with us were more adventurous than those using mainstream touring companies, and I found it astounding to hear how far they were prepared to go when looking for that unusual travel experience. Plans for our future tours always sparked discussion and sometimes triggered interest in possible destinations. We listened with fascination to Barbara and Bob Gray from Coffs Harbour talking about their bike-barge European adventure. Their joy of riding bicycles beside historic canals traversing lush rural countryside and away from crowded cities was evident. A beautifully restored canal barge hotel followed them and tied up each night where the only noises were cows mooing and water lapping.

This triggered our interest in visiting Europe, so in 2017 we decided to go. Lindy said, 'You never know what lies ahead, so let's do it while we can.'

At age sixty-four, I'd never been to England or Europe. How could this be when our travels kept us away from home for eight months in every year for the last thirty years? The answer? We'd just kept doing the same tours over and over again.

Old friends Ian and Shirl Salway, who also had never been to Europe, travelled with us. We flew out of Mascot on the 10th of June, 2017, and landed in Rome thirty hours later still on the 10th of June—Ian's seventieth birthday the whole bloody way. We toasted him before leaving Sydney and, with the time zone keeping up with us, again over the Indian Ocean, high above the Mediterranean and finally while enjoying a pizza for dinner in a back street of Rome, not far from the Colosseum.

Bruno and Christine gave very specific instructions on how to get from the Rome airport to our central hotel or, more specifically, how not to. We were tired and not very sharp, especially after all the birthday cheers, and I stupidly booked a bargain-priced hotel shuttle that jammed us into a van with fifteen other people and their luggage. About halfway to our destination, the van pulled into a petrol station and the English-speaking driver swapped with Omar, who then took us the long way to the hotel. An American travelling in the van disputed the fare and threatened the driver, so we intervened before punches were thrown. Even though Omar took us the long way to the hotel, he drove past the flood-lit Colosseum—one of the most magnificent sights we ever saw.

Following a couple of days exploring Rome, we caught a fast train up to Bolzano to meet up with Bruno and Christine as they passed through enroute to the Dolomites with one of their tour groups. Joining their tour group and seeing them in action for a few days filled us with pride as they took escorted travel to the next level—it was brilliant and a highlight of our lives.

Munich came next before driving to Obersalzberg to see the Nazi-era Eagles Nest high on top of a mountain in Austria. Unbeknown to Lindy and Shirl, Ian and I rented the biggest and fastest car we could get our hands on with the sole intention of going as fast as possible on the autobahns. I unleashed the big Mercedes to 200kph legally, but to our great amusement, Ian was booked for going sixty-five in a sixty zone later that same day.

In France we visited the Western Front to pay respect at the graves of my two great uncles killed in WWI, then to Brussels to board the MV Quo Vadis for a seven-day bike-barge tour ending in Bruges. We'd booked this online without any recommendation for that operator, but how lucky we were. Like Barbara and Bob, we had the time of our lives, seeing Europe from a bicycle and enjoying comfortable and sociable nights on board.

The *Quo Vadis* (Latin for Where are you going?) was a modified cargo barge built in 1939, just before WWII. When the Nazis invaded the Netherlands, the owner sank it to prevent its wartime use but with the intention of re-floating her one day. The diesel engine had been removed before scuttling in freshwater to hide it and minimise rusting. After the war she was re-floated and put back to work along the canals and rivers of Europe for sixty years before being converted into a very comfortable little floating hotel. The paint scheme of a royal-blue hull and white upper structure emphasised her beautiful classic shape with an upper-hull curve highest at the bow and dipping in an arc to the rear. She sat very low in the water to fit under low bridges and even had a collapsible wheelhouse to aid this process further so she could fit where many others couldn't. Onboard were twelve ensuite cabins, a restaurant, lounge bar and ample outside deck space and seating. What appealed most was the owner/operator shared our travel philosophy of avoiding touristy places whenever possible. The canal system, established before railways and roads, mostly wound through the rural landscape, connecting little villages away from the crowds.

People from Germany and Austria and two from the USA travelled with we four Australians on *Quo Vadis*, so German was the main language spoken on board. After dinner each evening, discussion took place in German about the following day's cycling activities followed by a very brief and hard to understand English translation. It didn't really matter, so we just enjoyed being disruptive and looking blank, shrugging our shoulders and cheerily answering 'yah' to everything. The ship's Dutch captain hosted a beer-tasting session one night and whatever he gave us to sample we clunked glasses, skulled it and said, '*Das gut.*'

Near the end of the trip, I walked past the wheelhouse and invited myself in for a chat with captain and owner, RJ—easier than saying his Dutch name. Charts lay in front of him and he was deep in thought, having just learned of a large group cancellation for the following year. I offered to help, and he was curious to know how because I told everyone on board I drove buses for a living. After a brief discussion, we shook hands on a deal giving us enough time to finish our European trip, get home and gauge demand with a newsletter.

After leaving *Quo Vadis* in Bruges, we caught a train to

London via the channel tunnel and joined a fourteen-day coach tour through England, Wales, Ireland and Scotland with a well-known and highly regarded company. The coach was new, hotels and meals were great, the driver was faultless and the guide was knowledgeable, very informative and pleasant—but the tour had no heart. It was simply industrial-scale tourism.

In Dublin, Lindy became unwell and spent twenty-four hours in hospital undergoing tests and observation. A nasty cycling buster in Europe had left bruises, and doctors were concerned about deep vein thrombosis issues but, to our relief, she was okay.

Back in Australia, we quickly promoted the canal barge tour and generated so much interest that we needed to book a second tour for 2018. It felt just like Canada all over again.

~

When at Sydney Airport the next year waiting for departure back to Europe, I noticed on our boarding passes that we weren't seated together, so I approached the desk in the departure lounge and raised my concern. I said my biggest worry was that my attractive wife might be seated beside someone better looking than me, and I couldn't take that chance. The staff at the desk chuckled and upgraded us to business class.

Quo Vadis was tied up in Amsterdam Harbour waiting for us, and RJ and his wife, Ina, welcomed us aboard like long-lost family. Together, we then welcomed all our Australian passengers—who arrived individually at the waterfront—and later hosted a meet-and-greet dinner. Afterwards RJ led the group on a walking tour of the city centre famous for its nightlife. I must've been tired because pastries displayed in the window of a Dutch bakery held more appeal than other 'products' blatantly displayed elsewhere. Next morning the vessel slipped the wharf, getting underway during breakfast, but soon all of us were up on the foredeck experiencing the remarkable seamanship with Captain RJ setting a course right through the city centre. He steered the fifty-five-metre-long vessel down narrow canals running right alongside busy city streets and under drawbridge decks raised just in time to let *Quo Vadis* pass under. The bridges lifted on cue like a perfectly choreographed play and eventually we noticed that a girl on a bicycle coordinated the whole procedure by riding from bridge to bridge just in time to stop the traffic and raise the decks. When realising this, some noisy passengers stood out on the front deck to cheer her onwards as she frantically peddled through the crowds and traffic to the next bridge.

Being back on *Quo Vadis* and preparing for some cycling through Europe again was like a dream come true, and we were determined to enjoy it to the fullest. The first day out of Amsterdam was unseasonably hot, but most of us were busting to get on the bikes and start the forty-five kilometres ride to Gouda where *Quo Vadis* would be waiting. With the hectic city of Amsterdam twenty kilometres behind, the barge stopped alongside the canal, and everyone got busy unloading bicycles and adjusting seats and helmet straps. The cycling guide, a Dutchman called Sietse, rode at the front, leading the way and setting the pace, while I rode at the rear to 'sweep' and make sure we left nobody behind. I grew frustrated within the first few kilometres when I noticed riders' lack of confidence and wobbling bums on seats. Soon this frustration turned to despair when I pondered the unlikely prospect of getting them all the way to Bruges in just ten days—at eight kilometres per hour. The effort was there, but their technique was just dreadful.

In the full heat of the day, we approached a pretty little

Dutch town, and the lady riding in front of me stumbled off her bike and collapsed to the ground complaining of dizziness. Nobody ahead saw this happen, so they kept peddling along into the town centre, leaving just the two of us about 500 metres behind. Locals came to our aid, getting her a cool drink and a shady place to sit, while I dashed into the town to get help, leaving her with caring strangers. My plan was to find either of the two 'Sallys' with the group, both of whom were registered nurses, and get either or both back to Pam. People going about their business filled the town's typical European market square, and I was frantic about ever finding a 'Sally' among the throng, but then I heard their loud voices and laughing coming from the other side of the square. They reacted promptly to my urgent plea, peddled back to Pam and attended to her very capably. One of the 'Sallys' was Lindy's younger sister, who has always possessed a charmingly strong voice. Sietse, the cycling guide, commented after a few days that she had a voice that 'rang out like the church bell'. Anyway, it was useful on that day at least.

After the incident we continued to Gouda where *Quo Vadis* was tied up close to the town centre. With us were Keith and Judith DeJong, who migrated to Australia from the Netherlands in their youth and were returning to their childhood land. Both toured many times before with us and often told us of their wartime hardships and childhood lives in the Netherlands. Keith was from Gouda, and he took us for a walk around his boyhood hometown, saying that little had changed since he left. The central market square looked like a scene from a storybook with its many narrow cobbled lanes leading into it from all directions. In the middle of the square stood a beautiful Gothic town hall dating back to the 1400s, and Keith led us inside and down a narrow stone staircase to a cellar where the Nazis held him captive for several days during the war. While in there we heard organ music coming from the nearby church, and he told how, before the days of electricity, it was his job to hand pump the bellows of that organ every Sunday.

After dinner aboard *Quo Vadis,* during the nightly evening announcements session, I raised the awkward issue of the dreadful bike riding. To introduce the problem, I drew on the wisdom of champion rugby league coach Jack Gibson who famously mangled the astute words of Henry Ford, saying, 'If you always do what you always did, you'll always get what you always got.'

To their great credit, and realising the need for change, they listened to Sietse's advice and, remarkably, the group's average speed lifted to nearly twenty kilometres per hour within days. My job as sweep became a 'gut bust' just to keep up, and I regretted not quoting Brian Smith, the perennial bridesmaid coach, to set their speed at a more comfortable fifteen kilometres an hour.

Cyclists preparing with Quo Vadis behind. Bruges, Belgium, 2017.

~

On all our canal barge trips, we visited the WWI battlefield sites of Flanders in Belgium and the Somme region of northern France. RJ steamed *Quo Vadis* down the River Leie to Wervik and tied up on the Belgian side of the river with France on the opposite bank. A bridge nearby made it easy to stroll over into the little French town of Wervicq-Sud with a history dating back to the third century and its Roman occupation. Having *Quo Vadis* located there gave us a perfect staging point for visiting the nearby Western Front battlefields, and like many people with heritage dating back a few generations in Australia, I had great uncles killed there during WWI. I knew how emotionally overwhelming the next few days would be visiting the fields, villages and towns within a short drive from there.

Whenever taking groups to places of great fame and significance throughout the world, thorough preparation enabled the best experience, especially here on the Western Front where emotions always overflowed to the point where most had a lump in their throat and teary eyes for days on end. With this in mind, we brought our professional battlefield guide, Duncan Barnes, aboard the night prior to discuss the plans, give information and answer questions. We already knew those with fallen relatives, having sought that information months before, and invited each one of them to personalise their family loss and tell what this visit meant to them. Duncan carefully planned each day around these people so they could visit the specific battlefield, understand the circumstances of the battle and pay respect at the grave site, if it was known.

After several days visiting historic sites, cemeteries and museums, the climax was attending the Last Post Ceremony held every night since 1928 (except during WWII) at the magnificent Menin Gate memorial in Ypres, Belgium. The memorial arch, built after WWI, stands where the old city gates opened out onto the ancient Roman road to Menin and through which the British and Commonwealth armies marched on their way to the Ypres Salient. Standing to attention under the memorial engraved with the names of 54,000 boys who had no known grave and listening to the music of bands or choirs from all over the world was overwhelming. For me, it was a time to give thanks and be grateful to be born at a time in history when I didn't have to farewell our sons to fight in a war on the opposite side of the world, like all those poor young boys with their names memorialised.

Later in the tour, Duncan met us again along with a coach and driver at De Panne on the southern coast of Belgium after our coastal tram tour from Oostende. The tram line ran down the English Channel coast for fifty kilometres past many resort towns and Nazi-era bunkers all the way to the French border. From there we travelled by coach to many of the sites made famous during the miracle 1940 evacuation of allied troops from the beaches of Dunkirk in France.

~

Quite a few of our personal friends joined us on *Quo Vadis* tours, including Max and Denise Cochrane. Max was a keen pilot but nearly killed me on a flight to the Orange National Field Days when we were teenagers. Denise rode her bike much the same as Max flew the Cessna as a young bloke. She was the only person who ever tried to remove a jacket over her head when cycling on cobblestones beside a canal. It can't be done! Luckily, we saw it happen and dragged her out of the water by the legs in a most unladylike way. Many friends accompanied

Max and Denise, including 'Clod' Emery, the group organiser who somehow accumulated a surplus of cash when organising, so was able to place three thousand Euros on the bar for the enjoyment of all. Captain RJ was initially alarmed at possible ramifications like people falling overboard, but the happiness was responsibly rationed over the next two weeks. My word, they enjoyed themselves.

~

One of the days most looked forward to was cycling to Arnhem, where *Quo Vadis* met us under the famous John Frost Bridge over the Rhine River. This was the focal point of the famous WWII battle, codenamed Operation Market Garden, where an attempt by the British to capture and hold this bridge failed when, despite their valiant attempt, reinforcements took too long getting there. That battle inspired the film *A Bridge Too Far*.

Vigorous discussion happened on the *Quo Vadis* the night prior to this special day on the two possible cycling routes to reach the bridge. We took a vote, and with a 50/50 split result, I volunteered to lead half via the Airborne Museum while the professional guide, Arie, took the remainder via a National Park and Art Gallery. My group's proposed route was unknown to me, so I planned to use Google Maps on my phone to find the way.

Next morning with the two groups all saddled up and ready to head off, I flippantly asked Arie to please not be late getting to the bridge because we were going to get there first and hold it until his group arrived to help.

My group enjoyed a most wonderful day with plenty of time for coffee stops and viewing the Airborne Museum, but when peddling out, we noticed Arie's group approaching from the wrong direction. They'd gotten hopelessly lost, ridden seventy kilometres and missed the National Park altogether. For them, that day was indeed a bridge too far.

Again, the experience with RJ and *Quo Vadis* was so happy that we booked for the following year. The circumstances leading us into regular European canal barge tours were so like those that led to North American tours that Lindy must have feared where it might be heading. She unambiguously told me NOT to buy our own barge.

On the long flight home from Europe in 2019 after the two barge tours, I sat beside a lady who occupied the aisle seat. She had very short hair, had no makeup and wore a sarong dress, so I thought she was a hippie. Soundly off to sleep she went all the way from Heathrow to Singapore, and I couldn't get out of my seat. When leaving the aircraft for a brief stopover at Changi, she commented how astounded she was that I hadn't stood up or gone to the washroom for the entire thirteen-hour flight. I casually replied, 'It's just mind over matter.' It turned out that she was a high-ranked Buddhist travelling to Australia to officiate at the opening of a temple in Brisbane. I think she was impressed, and we talked nonstop all the way to Sydney.

The year 2019 was our best year ever in both the personal and business sense, but January 2020 brought news of a virus spreading around the world from China. Within two days of hearing this, we were on a flight to Dallas TX to meet all service providers engaged for a tour in October and personally explain why we were deferring payments until June. The reason was our apprehension on how the virus might impact international travel. Maybe that was just lucky intuition, but soon the news broke of the *Diamond Princess* cruise ship being quarantined in Yokohama harbour, and fear gripped the travel industry at an alarming rate. Just days after getting home, tourism jolted to a stop in Australia and all around the world.

~

After eighteen months in lockdown and several failed attempts to restart touring, we accepted that the task of rebuilding was impossible without youth and energy. Throughout this time, we discussed, reminisced, laughed, cried, questioned, assessed and sought wisdom from friends and industry colleagues, but we just didn't know what to do. Our entire lives had been spent either leading tours or preparing for them, and we didn't want it to ever end. We never planned to be tour operators in the first place; life just steered us into it. The disciplined childhood on the farm and football field, inspiration to travel from other travellers, lessons learned through business setbacks, experience gained operating tractors and trucks and some very astute and timely advice all equipped us to do it.

Bruce and Lindy in 2019.

Very few people have been as lucky as us to have seen the sun rising from on top of Ayres Rock, heard the sea waves crashing at Galveston, climbed timber ladders to ancient Puebloan cliff dwellings, seen the great Arctic caribou migration, viewed New York City from the twin towers, toe-dipped in the Beaufort Sea and strolled across London's Westminster bridge hand-in-hand with the love of their life.

It was a privilege to do what we did for so long, meeting thousands of great people, making many lifelong friendships and accruing a wealth of precious memories. Best of all was that my love for Lindy grew even stronger when facing so many extraordinary experiences and challenges, side by side.

A verse of Robert Service poetry we saw painted on the wall of a dilapidated old building in Dawson City helped me to realise the inevitable.

> *I wanted the gold, and I sought it;*
> *I scrabbled and mucked like a slave.*
> *Was it famine or scurvy—I fought it;*
> *I hurled my youth into a grave.*
> *I wanted the gold, and I got it—*
> *Came out with a fortune last fall—*
> *Yet somehow life's not what I thought it,*
> *And somehow the gold isn't all.*

We have the wealth of family and a beautiful place to live at Shoalhaven Heads. Travel is what we do, but, from now on, it will be just the two of us towing a caravan.

As you would expect from a tour operator, I am busily researching and writing the itinerary.

Thanks, everyone.

Bruce Bishop

Tour Operator (Retired)

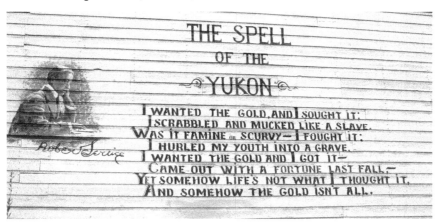

Lightning Source UK Ltd.
Milton Keynes UK
UKHW021403201222
414172UK00004B/6